Praise for *Blackbirds & My Boys*

Lisa's distinct, unique voice unapologetically sprinkles genuine bits of her soul—bruised and buoyed alike—throughout her Movements, giving the reader an intimate hand-holding to examine their own "bits." I often found myself reading, re-reading, then re-reading a descriptive passage simply for the pleasure of tasting it a few moments longer.

—Danica, editor and mother of three

Synopsis for *Blackbirds & My Boys*

Layering experiential imagery and emotional ink, Lisa's storied movements unravel raw the peculiar, frequently painful path of her slightly marginal life as a single mom imperfectly pursuing the heart of God with her three sons. With vulnerable honesty, Blackbirds and My Boys invites the reader into her own inward journey, traveling from opacity, rumination,and God-searching to destinations of clarity, peace—and being found by God.

Birthed from a deep immersion into familiar Scriptural texts, these evocative vignettes will tilt the reader's head for a fresh reframing of Sunday-schooled passages as Lisa reveals her struggles with juvenile diabetes and juvenile delinquency, with heroin addiction and God-eviction—and even a boyfriend-gone-bad.

Join Lisa as she discovers some beautifully bewildering blackbirds within the common commotion of her days and within the despairing darkness of her nights, where you are certain to discern a few blackbirds of your own!

Blackbirds & My Boys

MOVEMENTS FROM THE SOUL OF A MARGINAL MOM

LISA E. CURRY

For

Mama and Daddy,
the essential Blackbirds,

and

My Boys,
Taylor, Zach, and Sam

No words can capture how much I love you.

To
Diane, who envisioned a book
before I had even glimpsed a sentence.

For permission requests or for information regarding book orders and/or speaking engagements, write the author at BlackbirdsAndBoys@gmail.com.

Edited by Danica Patchen and Kelly M. Vaughan

Interior and Cover Design by Kelly M. Vaughan of Creative Gal LLC
CreativeGalLLC@gmail.com

ISBN-13: 9780692059210

Library of Congress Control Number: 2018901789
Lisa E. Curry,Omaha,NE

Printed in the United States of America

Contents

INTRODUCTION

I have wondered exactly when this book began, when all the rowdy thoughts and feelings of this socially inept, introverted mom bumped against one another within the warm waters of my awakening imagination before leaping out on paper in starched and ironed words.

The Movements which follow are simply short jaunts of discovery, finding grace and hope among the ordinary hiding places of life—and among the darker, harder-to-find spots within our often extraordinary struggles.

But also sheltered within these stories are your own stories. Really, they are all of our stories because they are all connected to the One Who holds our stories together: The beautiful feet-washing, donkey-riding God-Man.

Jesus.

My only prayer is that it is He whom you see, He whom you hear, and He whom you encounter as you read these words written with Him.

And, as my words become a blurry backdrop behind a stunning awareness of The Followed One, I am certain you will see, you will hear, and you will encounter the astonishing whoosh of beautiful blackbirds all around you.

Prologue

My God, *what is a heart*
That Thou shouldst it so eye and woo
Powering upon it with all Thy art
As if Thou hadst nothing else to do?

Mattens,
as quoted in *The Sacred Romance*

PRINCESS? *ME?*

The automatic doors at the emergency room entrance quietly slid open, an antithesis to my hammering heart and panicked breathing. I quickly found the partitioned unit where Taylor was lying, surrounded by hovering nurses and interrogating sheriffs. Glancing at Taylor, nausea threatened me as I assessed his face—bluish gray, freakishly distorted, and pummeled beyond my recognition. Nameless predators had beaten him so badly that truth had run scared from my son.

A CAT scan was ordered as I commanded my composure in this surreal reality. A reality where I could not scream "NO!" Where I could not scoop him up in my arms and run away. Away to the happily-ever-after of the countless books I had read to him as a boy.

After the test results had presented a thumbs-up for his release from the hospital, Taylor left with his father. And I headed home.

Alone.

Soundlessly I shut the front door. Shut the blinds. Shut out every reminder of reality. A reality where it seemed God had shut out me.

Me.

The only one He surely did not love. Crawling onto my couch and into the enticing darkness my shut-out world mimicked, I cynically murmured,

"Why *me?*"

But the strident ring of my cell phone invaded my time-abandoned cocoon like an unwelcome anachronism. Squelching its grating persistence, I answered, only to be assaulted by a harsher din of hurtful words. Words beclouding any stray shaft of light attempting to bravely rescue my despairing soul. Words which pointed an accusatory finger, painfully poking the pummeled face of my own heart.

Christmas was so close I could touch it, but I recoiled at its proximity, its impossible expectations groping for me as I stumbled through with watery eyes. Band-Aids from a recent break-up still clung to the fresh wound. Clients who once clamored to me for personal training had—in their undisciplined December—deserted me, too.

I wondered if there was an emergency room for my suffering spirit, a mystical hospital with soothing staff and inquisitive soul-searchers gently asking me,

Where had it so insidiously gone awry—my tender boy now an attacked teenager?

Why did I feel like a walking résumé, incessantly begging for a "Wow!"?

Who was I, this frenetic woman with low body fat and lower self-worth?

How could I continue in this vain chase, emptied in my panting pursuit of contoured emptiness?

For eighteen years I had gulped down daily doses of my worthlessness, which my marriage unfailingly spooned up. My voracious hunger for love had propelled me into a starvation cycle of hollow relationships emaciating my bulimic soul. Occasionally, during unbearable pangs of rejection—of deprivation—I had sensed God softly whispering and weeping, imploring me to crave Him, the One Who had picked and pursued me.

Yet I had ignored His hushed and haunting voice.

In my melancholy, make-shift shelter, memories tiptoed all around me. One was so faint and faraway, I questioned its sincerity. Two years had passed, but I remembered.

I remembered a familiar vibrancy moving within me. It had felt like the first kick of pregnancy when I first read the quote. The quote about discovering and doing that which makes you come alive. But after I had considered the absurdity of a passion-filled life, I rejected the impossible notion, suffocating the animated hope within me.

Yet I could not ignore the picture of my son's bruised cheeks, swollen face, and blackened eyes staring sadly at me in my mind.

I could not discount the heavy disconcertion smothering my spirit as the holidays dragged me along.

And I could not dismiss the invitation to join a group book discussion of *The Sacred Romance*. The idea of a love affair with God had seemed implausible, yet seductively irresistible.

Love-at-first-sight, it was not. Not for me, anyway. I was like a timid puppy, cowered in a kennel as an adoring new master coaxed me nearer, wanting only to quietly caress my face. Little by little, though, I moved closer and closer as God wooed me through poetry and music, through His Word and the words of those already captivated by His love, and through lakeside walks and windy days of an early blossoming spring.

Until one day—finally feeling safe—I allowed Him to pick me up and hold me.

Until one day, I said to God what He had been declaring to me all along.

"I love You."

A carefree courtship, it was not. I had had my doubts. Was it possible that the berated and belittled me was truly the beloved me? Deconstructing the embedded, bold billboards of lies—lies often corroborated by circumstances—I gradually grasped the delicate, fine print of truth.

Truth which had seemed too good to be true.

But God, well, He can be cleverly convincing.

———◆◆◆———

Heading out for a run one day, I had clicked on the television to check the weather. I was not expecting the scene—set in a garden during tea—from the movie, *The Princess Diaries*. I briefly watched with disinterest as Queen Clarise Renaldi, played by Julie Andrews, attempted to convince Amelia, played by Anne Hathaway, that she was a princess, an honest-to-goodness royal Princess. Amelia, flustered, denied the possibility of such a ridiculous assertion. Frustrated by Amelia's unbelief, Queen Renaldi told her she was a princess, whether she accepted it or not.

The next day, at a different time, I had turned on the TV to see the local forecast before running errands. Instead of a meteorological report, however, the exact scene from *The Princess Diaries* was playing out before me, beginning exactly where it had the day before. Perplexed at the unlikeliness, I watched hypnotically as the same dialogue between Queen Renaldi and Amelia unfolded.

Stunned, I clutched the remote, silent in this oddly holy moment, knowing that God had spoken.

He had spoken to me.

Me.

In my messy, unremarkable world that had survived a miserable marriage, a difficult divorce, and a multitude of mistakes,

I was—in a non-negotiable way—His Princess.

Clearly, however, Princess Me was not the pampered, problem-free royalty of girlish make-believe. Prince Charming had obviously been ousted to Never-Neverland; my far-from-majestic story, which included the battered face of a crown prince, lacked a happily-ever-after.

But there was one place in my story where my soul had recognized its regal splendor. I had discovered the secret sanctuary during one of my frequent walks around the lake. Surrounded by tall prairie grass, this concealed spot edged the backwaters where waterfowl played unnoticed. Where the wind enveloped and refreshed me, reminding me of God's presence.

On one particular afternoon while enjoying my private refuge, I was met with imagery so lovely. So loving. A woman, sitting on a bench, was sobbing, grieving over lost years never to be recaptured. Dancing blithely all around the weeping woman was a young girl, the ballerina I had once dreamed of becoming. Wind partnered with her giddiness, her laughter spinning so closely to the crying lady that her sadness was drawn into the girl's abandoned pirouette. And I could no longer distinguish between the two.

They had coalesced into one.

Me.

As a soothing breeze skipped across the lake, the submissive water cajoled the remorse of my past away from the shore in coruscating waves. Entranced upon this inviolable ground, even my shallow breathing seemed an intrusion.

Grabbing four rocks from the muddy bank, I surrounded the largest by three other rocks: my past, the innocent girl on the cusp of all she was created to be; my present, the mourning lady releasing all the ostensibly wasted, impotent time; and my future, a princess secured by Love in uncertain tomorrows. All these encircled the fourth Rock—the Nexus—God forever with me.

A sudden gust bent the grassy reeds framing my memorial while I, joining in their reverence, stretched my arms upward and offered an astonished,

"Why *me?*"

I returned often to those four rocks. When I craved His nearness. When I yearned for heaven and earth to blur together like the dancing girl and the weeping woman. Eventually, the crude rocks disappeared. I suppose shifting shorelines and wild weather were the thieves.

And though I have discovered other hidden havens where I can be alone as His princess—shut out from all but His luring light—the rudimentary altar remains in a safe spot.

My heart.

Movements

Before leaving the familiar landscape . . .
I wanted God to sketch out definite lines
so that I might know explicitly where I was going.
Of course, authentic faith eludes such certainty.
It means that we cannot cling to anything.
We must always leave something behind and not look back.
If we refuse to keep moving and insist on tangible proofs,
we diminish our faith, and that means unbelief.

Brennan Manning,
The Signature of Jesus

Go hide yourself by the brook Cherith . . .
I have commanded the ravens to provide for you there.

1 Kings 17:3–4 NASB

Scriptural References
1 Kings 17
John 6:68
1 Kings 18:34
Psalm 73:23–28

MOVEMENT ONE

Blackbirds

BLACKBIRDS

It was the third summer.

The third summer of our uncertainty.

The third summer of the manna, the constant reliance on the Invisible Love. Love which had often felt unloving. Un-good.

Summers were hard. I had grown disenchanted with the daily bread which had insisted upon daily dependence. My sons ate constantly, and they constantly ate away at my peace with their brotherly quarrels and appetites as insatiable as my anxiety. An anxiety which perpetually pestered me about providing my sons with new socks and new hope.

I had dropped out of grad school. The boys could not afford my nightly absences, and I could not afford the gas to commute there. Summa cum laude turned Loser. I was certain that the charred "L" branded on my brain had been seeping through my skin like an oozing odor, repugnant to anyone near me.

Augmenting my distorted distress was an ominous black hole in the cyber galaxy, sucking up every job application and résumé I had offered up to the unseen powers. Powers that separated the wheat from the chaff in the intimidating realm of employment.

Clearly I was chaff.

I had fantasized about becoming a savvy, fashionable career woman; in reality, even popular coffeehouses were unwilling to offer me a green apron.

I was trekking above tree-line, solo, with no supplies, no sighting of the summit. Was I just a frightened fool who had neglected precaution, wandering unaware off the easy, safe nature loop? Had I missed the trail marker warning the faint-of-heart?

Or was God absolutely real, and was He really coaxing me to climb this narrow ridge with only His hand to hold?

Short of breath, I had found myself parroting Peter's passionate words to Jesus,

"Lord, to whom else shall I go?"

All I had was God. And if God was God, He was completely in control of my out-of-control life. But if He was not, then truly I was as desperate as my Dad had declared me to be.

Desperate.

Certainly my life had seemed desperate. Fear followed me like a mangy stray looking for scraps, and I wondered if it would always stalk me. It was waiting for me that day I stared into my vacant refrigerator, which held only an abandoned apple and a few bottles of condiments guarding the solitary fruit like sentinels standing on the side.

And as I gazed into the empty icebox, I was reminded of the widow. The widow whose life had collided with Elijah the Prophet as she was stooped over gathering sticks by the gates of Zarephath . . .

> Her cupboards were empty too, save a bit of flour and oil, the ingredients for the last meager meal which she and her son would share together before their anticipated death. After all, for almost three years the drought had shown no mercy or immunity to its victims. The drought foreseen by the seer, Elijah.

> Elijah had been camping by a creek as King Ahab's kingdom dehydrated all around him. As starvation began to rob land and life, Elijah's groceries were delivered to him by ravenous ravens. Commanded by God's ironic grin, pillaging crows delivered bread and meat to Elijah twice a day.

> I wondered if Elijah had awakened—like I often did—with tautness in his stomach, uncertain if the black scavengers would devour his meals instead of delivering them. Yet the Unseen Goodness, Who caused crows to nourish Elijah, had likewise fed us.

> Always.

> Even as we—like Elijah, who watched a gushing brook become a desiccated ditch—panted for fresh

headwaters to fill our arid tributaries of ripped tennis shoes and fatherless voids, the blackbirds always came.

They came through Target gift cards slipped casually into my hand by friends or tucked into an encouraging card from Mama. Always unexpected. Always at my most urgent moments.

They came through a complete stranger who wrote me a check to train her for a race. She did not know my name nor did she know that I had been a personal trainer. I was completely broke on the day she approached me.

They came as I was pulling into our apartment parking lot, praying for weekend provisions. A fifty-dollar bill blew up right beside me as I opened my car door.

They came on a day when famine's foreboding sneer had drowned out the faint cawing of crows, and I was given a much-desired book. Taped to the inside of the book jacket was money for food, as if God had jumped out when I opened it, exclaiming, "Surprise!"

They came—unsolicited—through my dentist who offered her dental services free of charge.

They came after crying out to God while headed to church on Zach's thirteenth birthday—a birthday promising no presents or pomp—through congregants who stuffed hundreds of dollars into my empty hands during an Advent service. The pastor had decided, impromptu, to honor single mothers.

Yes, the blackbirds had come to me, too.

And Elijah had come to the despondent widow. The widow whom God had already instructed to feed him.

I wondered why she was preparing for her death when God had informed her she would be Elijah's hostess. But was I not this same husbandless woman, when my checking account reached the single digits? Did I not panic and begin collecting twigs?

Would He Who Maintains the Cause of the Afflicted cease from maintaining mine? How quickly I had forgotten the faithful blackbirds. How quickly I had forgotten their Guide, when I was running low on laundry detergent and laughter.

On cosmetics and courage.

On gas for my car and gratitude for the moment.

Was I not this same single mother looking down at the rain-deprived, cracked earth, not recognizing it was really a prophet's path? Not realizing it was the provocation to tilt my head upward to Living Water?

Was I not the same despairing mom—when confronted with the needs of others—who clenched her jaw, uttering,

"I have NO bread!"

Yearning for an elixir—for a comfortable salary and carefree independence—I could only see dry weather, diminishing necessities, and my sons starving for school clothes, famished for a father.

Like the slumped silhouette searching for tinder amidst bleak terrain, I was fueled by fear—raw fear—its raucous voice muffling the sound of returning crows, shrieking over the Voice Who had pledged provision . . .

Chilled by the cold air of the refrigerator, calculating how thinly to slice the last apple for the boys, I sighed deeply. Prayed deeply.

"How much longer, oh, God? How much longer must we struggle?"

It had seemed I needed to gather a few twigs and sticks for our imminent demise, but the widow confronted me in her own stark kitchen, her flour-dusted hands pointing to the brimming bowl and dripping jar.

The fragrance of her freshly-baked bread lured me into a truer reality: His Love will never leave, will never tire of my neediness; He revels in near-empty containers!

God did not simply postpone the deaths of a nameless mom and son. He had named her Not Forsaken. He did not simply supply survival staples to a lonely, despairing widow. He offered her significance, a kingdom cause bigger than her tiny, desperate world that had grimaced at tomorrow.

A worthless widow, a Gentile with nothing to give, was selected to be a giver, providing hospitality to one of the leading players in the biblical cast, Elijah.

Elijah!

Who had requested water again from another, this time not to quench his own thirst, but to drench a soon-to-be-scorched altar.

Elijah!

Who had shown up on the mountain with Jesus as He revealed His glory to a few disciples.

As I shut the refrigerator, I heard Him respond from a place as deep within me as my sighs and prayers.

"Would you be *My* voice, Lisa?"

His questioning answer was so unexpected. So startling.

So Him.

Could my confusing life, my starving circumstances, speak to another struggling soul, turning their downcast countenance upward to watch expectantly for blackbirds, to look gratefully at their Guide?

And I had replied.

"Yes."

Yes, to the same God Who had fed Elijah.

Yes, to the same God Who had filled the widow's empty canisters.

Yes, to the same God Who had sent the blackbirds to us.

Always.

. . . the faculty we have for receiving forgiveness
and the faculty we have for granting forgiveness
are one and the same thing.
If we open the one we shall open the other.
If we slam the door on the one,
we slam the door on the other.

N.T. Wright,
Evil and the Justice of God

Scriptural References
Luke 15:11–32

MOVEMENT TWO

Penny-Pinching Prodigal

PENNY-PINCHING
PRODIGAL

"**M**om, there is something I need to tell you."

The urgent distress in Taylor's voice immediately accelerated my heart and knotted my stomach. At 5:30 in the morning, I was barely awake as I settled into the driver's seat for our daily drive to the methadone clinic, where a quotidian dose of heroin replacement was dispensed for my son, preventing the harrowing effects of withdrawal.

Swallowing, I slowly met my eyes with his, finding both tears and terror. Uncertain at this half-conscious hour if I wanted to hear his divulgence, I cringed and hesitated before asking,

"What is it?"

"Honestly, Mom, I did not mean to do it. Last night I shattered the screen on your laptop when I closed it. I am so sorry. I had barely shut it, and I do not understand how it happened."

My pulse and tensed shoulders quickly dropped as I exhaled my relief. Relief that I was not a grandmother.

Yet.

Relief that Taylor was not an escaped fugitive accused of an unspeakable crime.

Yet.

My instantaneous appeasement was, well, instantaneous. Too soon my eyes were revealing tears, too.

The computer was inexpensive. Actually, it was the least expensive among the diverse selection of laptop technology. But my cheap keyboard and screen had not come cheaply to this frugal mom who had paid not merely the precious price of a couple of hundred dollars; the cost had demanded every thread of my safety net of precaution.

I had taken a dare.

A dare from God.

A dare to dream.

A dream to write.

And the laptop was my first scary step on the swaying, suspended bridge of God's double-dare.

Taylor interrupted my inattentive retrospection with his solicitation for my forgiveness. And, like an exemplar churchgoer, I dispassionately articulated that he was forgiven before requesting silence during the remainder of the trip.

Silence.

But it was not silent. Though it was quite quiet in the car, my suspicious thoughts were very vocal, loudly accusing Taylor of carelessness—of lying—before nimbly naming me as the culprit. A culprit who should not have shared her treasured laptop.

When we arrived home, Taylor repeated his apology, thanked me for understanding, and hugged me as he went into his room for some extra sleep. While he napped, I discovered the lacerated laptop abandoned on the couch. I approached it slowly, as if it were a gruesomely bloody body from a crime scene. Carefully picking up the victim, I examined the damage before contacting a few computer experts to discuss repair. Their unanimous consensus was that my prized possession was not worth the investment required to fix the screen. And my discouragement and dismay speedily switched to an inner disdain, scorning Taylor for his reckless handling of my computer, and again, deriding my careless self.

My self-derision, however, was no longer due to the second-guessing of my laptop loaning. It was regret.

I had not honored my end of the dare.

I had not written one word.

Because Taylor was spending the summer with me while his dad underwent a stem-cell transplant, I had blamed my breach on the distractions of pre-dawn wakeups, erratic schedules, and constant conversations with Taylor. My brainy, book-loving son had returned, pervasive personality and all, re-tethering a long-lost link.

Yet somewhere during this overdue connection, I had detached from the dare which I no longer believed I could—or should—fulfill. My dreams, impatient and sulking, had packed their bags for a distant country. Perhaps God, in reconsidering my neglect, had reciprocated, reneging on our venture.

And my useless, splintered screen seemed to echo my sequitur.

When Taylor awoke, he was happily back to his usual banter. Morning's morose son had incredibly recovered, without a syllable about the computer casualty.

He acted as if nothing had even happened.

And an unsettling irritation, like skin slowly chafing on a hot-weather run, rubbed red within my spirit.

Had I expected more contrition and less levity? More mea culpa for the loss I had suffered at his hands? Hands which were not groveling with offerings of atonement? The burden of proof—proof of his repentance—was on his relaxed shoulders. Shoulders which bore no evidence of lingering penitence.

My shadowy expectations of Taylor ambushed me, ripping off my doctrinal undergarments and exposing my private, duplicitous parts before God.

God.

The eager Papa Who replaces my tattered clothes with a pretty party dress and hires a caterer and acoustic ensemble when He first glimpses my returning, repentant heart.

Why then, when confession called me home, did I refuse to feast and dance, choosing instead to slouch against the porch, slinking away from His outstretched hand inviting me inside as the guest of honor? I acted as if God required groveling with offerings of atonement, proofs of contrition borne on shoulders bent under the heaviness of my remorse. And here I was, cast as the Incarnation, yet playing the devil's advocate, presuming Taylor should playact my gospel-less performance while I substituted the splintering cross for dramatizations of compunction.

I had become the false god I had crafted, not the mercy-saturated Jesus I was asked to imitate.

Not the delighted Daddy Who throws an outrageous homecoming party just for me.

For Taylor.

Taylor, my son who had returned home temporarily to me.

My son who apparently had apprehended the fleshing out of forgiveness far more than my far-from-free heart.

So I pulled myself up from this purgatory-like porch I had conjured and crafted, pausing to collect my confidence before grabbing the front door handle. But before my soul was fully standing, God swung the door wide open! And His laughter was peeling louder than the disco beat inside where Taylor was already dancing! Handing me a plate of freshly grilled veal, He welcomed me with an exuberant embrace and told me to make myself at home.

He acted as if nothing had even happened.

So I made myself at home, scavenging around until I discovered an old computer monitor. After dusting it off, I hooked it up to my crippled laptop, now a makeshift desktop.

And I began to write:

"Mom, there is something I need to tell you . . ."

You're blessed when you're content
with just who you are—no more, no less.
That's the moment you find yourselves proud owners
of everything that can't be bought.

Matthew 5:5,
The Message

Scriptural References
Matthew 5:1–12

Tenderfoot

TENDERFOOT

Oblivious to his striking features, Zach, at sixteen, was probably about two inches taller than he appeared. Skinny as spring asparagus, he usually had his shoulders bent, hands stuffed in denim pockets. Except for hitting golf balls at the driving range, Zach has never had any interest in any activity involving a ball, has never played on a team.

Zach arrived on this planet with an odd serenity, attentive and quiet after a brief, obligatory yelp. When he was barely crawling at his one-year check-up, the doctor—with a mixture of pity and piety—proclaimed my beautiful, blue-eyed baby would never be a star athlete. Maybe that was why sports had always been superfluous to Zach.

I had never coerced my sons onto a football field or a baseball diamond. I had never participated in the sorority of soccer moms. I had never cheered on sore rear from uncomfortable bleachers, nor cringed sympathetically at uncomfortable blunders. It had seemed my three budding men missed an integral developmental stage—unless you count the one occasion that Zach went to a golf team practice in junior high. By the second practice, however, Zach had refused to get out of the car.

Emulating his big brother, Sam, my youngest son, had stubbornly walked home without placing his foot on the track I had dropped him at for summer running camp. In retrospect, he probably got the better workout that day.

Zach had pulled a similar stunt. Though I had acquiesced to his athletic atheism, I was not so graciously tolerant of his disinterest in church youth group. After all, God had certainly expected me to strong-arm Zach into enthusiastic, transformational involvement in this necessary high school milestone.

Following the precedent of his golfing career, Zach had attended one get-together, hosted in an affluent neighborhood, attended by car-owning teenagers who, unlike Zach, were not driven to this spacious home by their mother. Following the chili-in-a-bag-of-Fritos, the kids were divided into groups according to their favorite football team. Unfortunately, there had not been a group for enlightened teens who had not joined the ranks of sports-infatuated masses, and who could hold discussions free of football metaphors.

Zach had wondered where God was that evening.

Adamant that Zach give youth group another chance, I threatened him into the car for round two of my impassioned compulsion. Actually, it was round two of a fighting match. After too many minutes, he very reluctantly stepped out of the car, and I quickly pulled out of the driveway, speeding away into the cold, rainy night.

And although I had not known it, Zach had done the same. Except he had not sped away.

He had walked.

I was completely nonplussed when Zach had finally arrived home, wet and weary. Attacking his downright defiance, I had militarily issued a punitive consequence before ordering him straight to his room.

But I could not fall asleep that night.

What would cause a couch-loving gamer to trudge a dark and damp distance, minimally dressed for the nippy temperatures? More importantly, what would drive a God-loving mother to force her tender, not-a-poser teen into the mandatory membership of a clique cloaked in Christianity?

A desire for Zach to experience vibrant community?

To expand socially and spiritually?

To encounter a father-like mentor for that father-hole in Zach's world?

Yes.

Yet it was much more. I could not hide from the shadowy provocateurs lurking beneath my mom-of-the-year veneer. From the not-so-noble motives of my fervent insistence. I was operating under the intoxicating influence of garbled assumptions, believing that I was complying with what was expected—no, required—in Christian parenting. Indeed, the vaporous dissent of others was wafting near if I neglected this essential force-feeding of church culture to my church-shunning sons.

Distorted underneath that skewed perspective was God—or, rather, a god—disappointed and incredulously shaking his head as he handed me my parenting report card marked with harsh, red "F's." Beneath that, however, was my blushing heart, yearning for a satisfying, deep belongingness for me and my boys. An organic sense of family that just happens without completing forms or auditioning for a part.

Exposed, too, was my weariness. Weariness from fighting too many battles alone. Frenzied from fighting like a lone general with a dull sword, screaming for reinforcement only to realize the troops had gone AWOL. Maybe that was why I had longed for their involvement in sports—a sort of organized, trained brigade to assist me in my warfare.

———◆———

Shortly following Zach's rebellious hike, he had called me from the nursing home where he worked part-time after school, asking me if I could give Marge a ride home. I had agreed immediately, not knowing who Marge was or where she needed to go. I only knew that this was important to Zach.

When I arrived for pickup, Zach was walking behind an elderly woman wearing the same purple scrubs which Zach wore. Underneath her hairnet was a tired face, familiar with hard work. Plopping down in the passenger seat beside me, she immediately began talking, disclosing her pay rate, marital history, and the geographical dots on the map of her seventy-year life as we drove the ten miles to her daughter's home, now her own. Money was tight, as it had been all her life, and it was obvious from her unfiltered, matter-of-fact monologue that she had never questioned the hardness of her life.

It just was.

Exiting the car with a kind and quick thank-you Marge disappeared inside her front door. I turned to Zach, sitting quietly in the backseat. Smiling, I praised him for his helpfulness to Marge.

"Mom, Marge told me that she was just going to walk home. That is a long walk for anyone, especially her age. I could not let her walk home—I just couldn't. And I knew you wouldn't mind bringing her home. Thanks, Mom."

What gentleness! What compassion! In one moment Zach had just scored one hundred touchdowns at the football game I never had to attend.

He had won the golf tournament well under par without putting one stroke.

He had demonstrated the intended fruits of consuming one hundred bags of Fritos with chili!

It had seemed God was winking at me as He whispered,

"Blessed are the gentle."

And in that humbling, heartening moment invigorated by a fresh blast of hope heightened by clarity—I knew.

It was not up to me.

God is, after all, God.

Not me.

Not sports.

Not organized church activities.

Only God.

God Who hears the prayers behind a mother's anxious duress.

God Who knows the silent aching of a teenage son's heart.

Of Zach.

Zach, whose grades had appeared average at the next parent-teacher conference. Average, until we spoke with his history teacher. As soon as we took our seats in front of him, my intuition told me he liked Zach. His comments proved me correct.

"With a little more effort, Zach has what it takes to make an 'A.' But Zach does something that most of my other students do not. Zach treats everyone, especially me, the way that others should be treated. I can't say that to too many parents or I would be lying. Zach treats me the way I should be—the way I like to be—treated."

My breath caught as my eyes misted over. Jesus' mountainside words were echoing through the noisy atrium filled with parents and their teenagers. But it was my son—my son—whose life was shouting His message.

I expressed my appreciation for his sincere compliment, wondering if he had recognized their profundity. As I rose from the folding chair to shake his hand, I realized that one hard, metal chair was better than one hundred bleachers.

Way better!

We never saw Marge again. She had quit a few days after I had met her. They had cut her hours at work, and her cost in gas exceeded the benefits of working the reduced hours. But the tenderness of a sixteen year-old young man named Zach was a soft cushion to her hard life.

Blessed are the gentle, for they bless those who have not been treated gently.

Like Marge.

Now faith is the assurance of things hoped for,
the conviction of things not seen . . .
And without faith it is impossible to please Him,
for he who comes to God must believe that He is and
that He is a rewarder of those who seek Him.

Hebrews 11:1, 6 NASB

Scriptural References
Mark 2:1–5
Luke 2:41–51

Our
Sam, My Sam

HOLY SYRINGES!

It was the first day of school.

The first day at a new middle school where Sam was starting eighth grade. Rushing Sam along, I had thrown on some old running shorts and a sweat-stained tee shirt, ignoring my porcupine hair. I checked if Sam had given himself his shot before we headed out on this bright, full-of-promise morning.

He had not.

And would not.

Grabbing the vital vial and syringe, I had directed him to the car, assuming I would administer the injection when we pulled up for drop-off.

My assumption was false.

Sam swiftly slipped out of the car before I had reached a complete stop. I jumped out of the car, rapidly closing the gap as he glared back at me.

We were—on this morning of expectant beginnings—in our sixth year of accommodating the inexorable demands of this unremitting invader. At first, Sam had surrendered, and he quickly adapted to the rigorous life of a seven-year old boy diagnosed with juvenile diabetes. But somewhere amid innumerable finger pokes, countless carbohydrate calculations, too many middle-of-the-night checks, and inestimable painful pricks from shots, compliance morphed into defiance.

And Sam was incessantly scared his blood sugar would drop too low.

I was uncertain when this fearful fixation began to consume him. Maybe it had started at summer camp for diabetic kids, where spooky tales of seizures were whispered around the campfire, igniting a wildfire of panic in Sam's pounding heart.

He was terrified.

Terrified.

That was exactly how I had felt years earlier when Sam had arrived via ambulance at the emergency room with labored breathing and relentless vomiting. When the brusque ER doctor had announced flatly that Sam might not make it, it was *my* heart beating violently that day. The day this unexpected intruder had arrived, masquerading as an intense intestinal flu, which I wished it would have been.

Lying beside Sam in the children's intensive care unit that night, numb, I had stared pensively at my son. Sam would survive, even though my completely carefree boy would not. From eating to sleeping, from school to play, life with—and for—Sam would never be the same.

Yet my sobering acceptance in ICU could have never predicted this let's-make-a-good-impression-on-the-first-day-of-school scenario. Me—wild eyes and wilder hair, dressed for yard work—chasing after my son with hypodermic in full view of gaping students and freaked-out faculty. Faculty who immediately accosted and escorted us into the principal's office where I would spend the entire morning, meeting all the staff, lunchroom workers included, explaining the complexity and perplexity of Sam's resistance to treatment—all while nervously attempting to mash down my uncooperative hair.

Undoubtedly, after studying my appearance, they were not the least bit surprised by these issues.

Issues which had already catapulted us to numerous therapists, most to whom Sam had refused to speak.

Issues which had led to his hospitalization—shortly following this eighth-grade debut—where he had befuddled the nurses by sneaking out to the snack room. A lot.

Issues which had caused me to chain-up cabinets and refrigerator, issue job cards, withhold the internet, scream in frustration, and weep in despair.

Issues which had impacted Zach.

Sam.

And me.

I had accepted Sam's diagnosis like a lead-weighted baton which God had passed off to me before He had taken a seat in the bleachers, semi-sympathetically watching as I ran robotically with this non-transferrable heaviness clenched in my hand. I had wondered often if He—way up in the nose-bleed section— had even heard my feeble cries for help.

I felt as if the trajectory of Sam's health—Sam's life—completely hinged on my performance in this one-man relay.

Somewhere between painful pokes and perpetual pricks— between carb counting and clutching control—my God-reliance had morphed into unconscious defiance.

Never had I even considered asking God to heal Sam.

My anaerobic compulsion had deflated God and suffocated hope in my oxygen-depleted heart. A God Who could quicken life in man and womb had mutated into a god who had no power to resurrect a boy's pancreas or his skeptical, scared spirit. And it had seemed safer to wheeze and gasp, sprinting away from embryonic disappointment. But I had not felt safe at all.

I was exhausted.

I had really wanted to trust God as the One Who cared deeply about the ceased secretions of Sam's insulin and the cynicism of his soul.

The God Who was, well, God. My God. Sam's God.

So I handed the heavy baton back to God. Hands freed and empty, I removed the roof of my egocentric faith. No longer panting breathless, I had imagined lifting Sam onto a pallet, and slowly, steadily, lowering Sam to Jesus.

And for an ephemeral moment—a moment so fleeting I had doubted the image—I saw Sam. I saw Sam smiling his Sam-smile, a restrained half-smirk threatening to bust out into a full grin. Though I could not see Jesus, I knew that Sam had. His happy face was free of fear . . .

<hr />

It was the first day back at school.

High school.

Christmas break had ended, and Sam's blood sugar was extremely high when he had awakened on this cold, "It's a new year!" morning. He, of course, was annoyed at my concern. His diabetic check-up the day before had been a wash; unwilling to reveal the extent of his yuletide eating without treating, he had intentionally forgotten his meter readings.

When we pulled up to the school for drop-off, he mumbled an agitated "love you," before disappearing among the arriving students. As I was pulling away, I glimpsed discouragement loitering by the curb, sneering at me as he mouthed,

"Nothing's changed."

Glancing back at the fading phantom in my rearview mirror,

smoothing my unruly hair, I answered.

"Yes, something has changed. *Me.*"

And Grace, beautiful Grace, is changing Sam, too.

Because we are—on this morning of expectant beginnings—hoping.

Hoping for that which we cannot yet see.

RESURRECTION!

She had been fighting back tears from the moment we sat down, and her startling demeanor was like a sledgehammer to the dam which had denied my own tears. But instead of launching into her summation of Sam's progress for that quarter—like every other teacher had done during this first parent/teacher conference of Sam's senior year she only repeated one thing.

"Sam!"

That had certainly been the exclamation trumpeting from every one of Sam's teachers on this revelatory evening.

"Sam! He is brilliant, creating computer applications which I had never imagined possible!"

"Sam! He has exceeded my own understanding of this subject!"

"Sam! I want him to return and lecture my class while he is in college!

"Sam! He is a leader, always helping other students with the material!"

And now, here we sat in front of his AP Psychology teacher, her brimming eyes matching my own heart, so filled up with shock and awe and gratitude that it threatened to spill out on the gray tiled floors. As she spoke of having had Sam as a fledgling freshman—and a failing one at that—she had expressed her amazement at how far Sam had come. At who he had become.

Finally, the liquid emotion escaped from our best intentions, and the parent/teacher conference became more like a parent/teacher cry fest. And Sam, my emotion-eschewing, praise-spurning son, was mildly mortified, his turned-away face as red as the school's team color.

And my turned-upside-down feelings were as yellow as a smiley face, as unexpected as a miracle on a mundane day. No teacher's amazement had exceeded my own. Especially considering that over the past three years, Sam had spent more time in the nurse's office than the classroom, his detached disinterest reflected in his barely passing grades.

Yet, here in this familiar folding chair, I was confounded by my own son's success, still gaping from the stunning remarks from all his teachers. Certainly this must have been how Mary had felt, in part, when, in an unimaginable, seventy-two-hour panic, she had finally found Jesus, post-Passover, sitting calmly in the temple among the religious teachers, teachers more dumbfounded than Sam's . . .

> Jesus was twelve. Half-boy, half-man, he had just participated in His first Passover, a rite of passage for all Jewish males His age, an age on the tipping point of obligation. An obligation to observe

the commandments, to contribute to religious services. But Jesus was not quite thirteen when Mary—a study of immeasurable relief, angry frustration, and flabbergasted fascination—had discovered her Son, listening and probing and answering the awestricken rabbis.

And the scholars in the temple courts must have been equally taken aback by Mary, an overwrought harridan shockingly showing up—and speaking up—at the men's club, crazed and sleep-deprived from a seven-day celebration and a three-day search party.

They had never expected such a detour, Mary and Joseph. Happily drowsy as they headed back to Galilee following the festivities, they—clearly not hovering control-freaks—had traveled for an entire day supposing that their perfect, albeit MIA, Son was with them.

He wasn't.

With a slight lurch in their stomachs, they had begun shouting His name, hunting and hounding among cousins and aunts and uncles and friends until, sickened and hyperventilating, they turned back, their desperation mushrooming with each caravan they encountered, frantically looking for their lost Boy—all the way back to Jerusalem.

And on the third day, after doggedly searching among lingering pilgrims—their voices rasping, their hope waning—they had spotted Him. Paralyzed by their perplexity, they had stared and staggered, only half-recognizing their Boy. Their Boy Who had studied, since a young Lad of four, under some of the most educated, famous, and passionate Jewish teachers. Their Boy Who had shared in the vibrant religious communities of Galilee, their rich discussions and lively debates pulsating within His young spirit.

Yet, in this clock-less moment of bewilderment, they had wondered if He was really theirs at all. And when Mary snapped to, as if a spell had been broken, her stern words marched out double-time, a hoarse, jarring stampede interrupting the erudite discussion.

"Son!"

"Why have You treated *us* like this?"

"Your father and I have been anxiously searching for You!"

Words were tumbling excitedly from Sam's Psychology teacher, too, as she shared with me about an assessment which Sam had recently taken—a challenging assessment placing Sam in the 100th percentile while most students had scored in the 50th percentile. And her disclosure came to me like an abrupt awareness, like a whiplashing of my neck as I checked on Sam, only to discover that the Sam I thought I knew was nowhere near.

Somewhere in between high school and Dairy Queen shifts and closed bedroom doors and geeky friends and computer fixations—and a beautiful girlfriend—he had slipped away. Or maybe he had had not slipped away at all. Perhaps I had trekked back on the same trail, thoughtlessly assuming he would stay close to my side, and Sam had simply remained, tipping over to the other side of that point.

His pulling away, I had felt it. Painfully. Yes, Sam had, at times, been harsh and hurtful. Mostly though, he had been an adolescent male, stretching closer and closer to manly obligations. Closer and closer to his unique individuality. And as I sat—suspended in this surreal twinkling of life, its reality anchored by table and teacher—I knew that my words, my heart, had too often echoed Mary's.

"Sam!"

"Why have you treated *me* like this?"

I was still a pool of emotion as Sam and I walked across the parking lot, side-by-side and quiet, the school's concrete beams guarding the holy ground inside. Shutting the car door, I looked at Sam. He was already shaking his head, as if to stop the applause about to bounce off my tongue.

Shaking his head, as if to ask why I had been so surprised.

But Jesus, He had not merely gestured the question. He had spoken it. Unapologetically.

Unequivocally.

"Didn't you know?"

Something had shifted following Jesus' first Passover, it seemed, a sentience of His vocation honing laser-like ahead. Sam had that, too. Already being paid well for ethical hacking, already considering an internship with a computer consultant, Sam was in single-minded pursuit of his passion.

Didn't I know?

I imagined the key scene, the distinguished rabbis as baffled and speechless as this distraught couple had been when they had stumbled upon this surreal gathering with Jesus. And Jesus had befuddled them all even more when He announced,

"I had to be in My Father's house."

My Father's house?

Had not this whole ordeal unraveled, not in the humble home of the stupefied man staring incredulously at all of them, but in the temple of the unspeakable Yahweh?

Though muted and mystified, surely Joseph had felt a paternal pang as his adopted Son's emphatic words punctuated this bizarre drama like a stinging reminder, like a not-so-subtle cue for Joseph to release this Boy he had loved and raised and wrestled playfully with. To let go of his fatherly responsibility for the actions of Jesus, a Boy-Man on the cusp of thirteen.

Yet there stood Joseph, as puzzled as his outspoken wife, but as silent in this passage as he was throughout all the gospel accounts.

Silent.

Sam's dad had also been silent. But it was a very different sort of silence. The sort of silence which had spoken no blessing. Still, in spite of this unwanted void, Sam was becoming—well—he was becoming Sam.

When we had returned home, I was still clutching the papers from the conference, each page a book full of grace. I read them through again, my eyes still watery, my spirit still worshiping. Reluctantly, I slipped them inside a drawer.

But I pondered them in my heart for a long, long time.

They began to relate their experiences on the road,
and how He was recognized by them
in the breaking of the bread.

Luke 24:35 NASB

Scriptural References
Matthew 5:3
John 6:53
Luke 24:13–35

Road Experiences

ROAD EXPERIENCES

Voice and violin dismantled the sanctuary's rooftop as worship ascended, melding clock-bound congregants with the Eternal Holy. As I lifted my face upward, a woman, two rows ahead of me, pulled my eyes off-center. Restricted only by her allotted pew space among the just-woke-up grungy and the dressed-in-Sunday's-best, she danced unabashed, her wildly waving arms swaying high above unkempt hair and frumpy tee shirt—a formless freestyle of pure joy.

My southern upbringing nudged me as I reflexively assessed her with a "Bless her heart."

Words of grace from Galatians were released, like hundreds of hovering butterflies greeted by her occasional, exuberant "Amen," as if she had delightedly caught one of the elusive, winged creatures. In moments when the outrageous gospel-goodness resonated within my divided focus, her unhindered hands would shoot up like happy, helium balloons.

My arrogance tapped me on the shoulder and suggested she could not possibly understand the message.

As the Sunday service culminated with Communion, the elements of Eucharist devoured my disciplined demeanor and theological savvy as I, enthralled, watched her dunk a wedge of crusty bread into the pewter cup of garnet wine, her smile so wide it barely fit her ageless face. Approaching the torn loaf as I lined up behind her, I—as Jesus told us we must—remembered . . .

The unadorned, warm baguettes had always worn that freshly-baked fragrance that dared us to resist. And we never did. My boys and I would file into the upscale bakery-café, our eyes and appetites lingering over the showy, colossal cookies and high-top gourmet muffins, fully aware that their price tag multiplied by four would exponentially surpass our dollar-and-some-pocket-change budget.

Feigning disinterest in the enticing array of sweets, we would matter-of-factly place our order for one of their fabulous loaves of French bread, and, after grabbing several butter packets, we would head to a back booth to devour the chewy, yeasty feast. As we slathered butter on every crumbly bite, we scarcely noticed the epicurean delights being consumed by the chic patrons around us.

Sam was three.

Zach was six.

Taylor was ten.

And I was surviving.

The boys' father, then my husband, had left us at an acquaintance's home in Paradise Valley, Arizona after we had driven straight through from Asheville, North Carolina. I had been told that we could stay there if the abuse escalated to intolerable.

It had.

Standing like refugees in their driveway—suffocating in the oven-like heat, clinging to a couple of suitcases—we watched as the boys' father pulled away from the palatial mansion of this family we barely knew. Abandonment was strangling me as I gulped the dry, hot air, refusing to cry.

Pretending to smile.

Staying to escape the unbearable.

But rigid rules and strict schedules dwelled within the luxurious surroundings of this impeccably mannered and perfectly attired family. It was a house of glass edicts, begging to be shattered by my free-spirited boys. Compliance was not optional, and I constantly feared a severe citation, especially from the lengthy list of laws for the dining room, posted like Luther's 95 Theses above the table. I had dreaded mealtimes.

One evening during dinner, Sam, a carrot-lover, had eagerly forked up a hefty mouthful of a healthy-but-horrible carrot salad; after tasting it, however, he spat every shred of orange across their lovely table.

Certainly that was the moment my hair had begun to gray.

Bedtime, once a laborious struggle, solicited no protests from my boys. They, too, had absorbed the tiptoeing tension. Shutting the door to our bedroom at night—as the boys unrolled their sleeping bags—the muscles of our souls relaxed, our taut spirits exhaled.

One night, after our whispering had dwindled into quiet breathing, faint sobs jostled me from half-asleep to wide-awake. Fumbling along the floor, I traced the tears to Zach, my little Tenderfoot, as my Dad had affectionately nicknamed him.

I barely breathed as I stroked his hair the way he loved, softly asking him what was wrong.

"I don't know, Mom. It just doesn't feel good here. It just doesn't feel good."

His childlike precision painfully pierced me, emancipating all my imprisoned tears as I gently agreed.

It did not feel good.

Occasionally we were allowed to borrow one of their

cars, and, having lost the liberty to order my day and freely go as I pleased, it felt like an exhilarating jail break. Perhaps it was during our release that their children would be exhorted—as I was later told by their mother—that my boys served as a reminder of whom they must never become.

After all, each of my boys had speech impediments while their children were being trained to become articulate guests at the White House.

Thrilled with our independence, our happy picnics of humble baguettes and creamy butter were welcome windows of revelry; we giggled hysterically as we ate, occasionally spilling water without reprimand. We felt like a family again, content in merely being together, ungoverned and uninhibited . . .

As crumbs and grapey sweetness lingered on my tongue, God elbowed me and whispered,

"Blessed are the poor in spirit. My kingdom is theirs."

I should not have needed the reminder.

God's handprints of goodness had been liberally smeared over our desert sojourn, gracing us with a paucity that found kingdom food appealing—satisfying—and favoring us with a hunger that relished the sacred serendipity of simple bread.

Impoverishment had been the vehicle which had driven us to His table, and it had transported me this day, empty-handed and broke, to where pocket change was worthless currency. Where I stood level with all who ate His body and drank His blood, agreeing that otherwise, I had no life.

Only the unpossessed can possess His kingdom.

Can feast on Life in abandoned dance.

I stared at the beautifully carefree woman one last time, her fashion-snubbing indifference and loud outbursts winking at me.

"Keep me poor in spirit, Father," I prayed.

When I turned to leave the church, I imagined her chasing after me like a child running out for recess, pulling my arm, and breathlessly exclaiming,

"Bless *your* heart!"

Confession is the Emancipation Proclamation for the soul. And it is our nudity which inspires nudity.

Lisa Curry,
Blackbirds & My Boys

Scriptural References
Matthew 8:18–22
Mark 5:21–34
1 John 1:8–10
Matthew 5:8
John 4:5–42
Psalm 18:16, 19
John 19:28
John 8:1–11, 32

Undressed by Naked Women

FEMININE PROTECTION

I was curled up cozily, reading as I window-watched fall's dance outside, trees swaying on chilly stage, their colorful trinkets teased by wild wind before escaping like runaway children from their mother's loose hold. And I wondered—if I were an oak or an aspen in autumn—could I so easily relinquish my golden offspring opulently displayed against turquoise sky?

Would I cling franticly to the enviable beauty that dressed my barren branches?

I returned to the story that had captured my attention that crisp morning—a story told by Matthew and Mark about a desperate, hemorrhaging woman. Her hellish menstruations, her chronic anemia, I shared this common bond with her. Yet her unceasing twelve-year struggle had offered no three-week recovery programs.

No comfort of companionship.

This nameless pariah, contaminated and contagious, had been sentenced to one hundred forty-four months in a prison of loneliness, banished to isolation.

Never touched.

Never touching.

Four thousand, two hundred, irrepressible days of shedding dignity.

Shedding hope.

Until the day when Jesus, surrounded by the smothering, chaotic crowds, collided with a man who fell, clinging to His feet.

A man as despairing and resource-void as the bleeding lady who was watching from the fringe, listening to his forceful, frightened plea on behalf of his dying daughter—a girl whose days had spanned the length of the woman's incessant bleeding. A girl on the precipice of womanhood and its monthly demands of blood.

But when the pitiable, bleeding woman spotted the edge of Jesus' robe moving in and out of the sweating, pressing bodies barricading her from the Man Who Heals Dying Daughters, she was stunned by what she had dared to imagine.

What she had dared to believe.

Forcing her frail, exhausted body through the thick pool of people, stretching toward Jesus as her lungs gasped for air, her shaking finger finally brushed the rough fabric cloaking her only remaining Possibility.

And immediately, a foreign vitality invaded her once-depleted veins.

The relentless, repugnant discharge had ended.

And she was terrified.

"Who touched Me?"

Fearfully, she cowered at the command of the Curer's words.

Words which had instantly halted the crushing throng, their loud cacophony muted as they now glared down at her. Expecting condemnation from the Man she had made unclean, she flinched as His gaze found her, cringing and completely exposed.

Now salient among the faceless onlookers, once an object of contempt, this woman courageously confessed everything.

Everything.

She confessed everything in front of everyone.

Everyone.

I peered at her through the curious, condescending crowds, maintaining a safe distance from this woman. Once completely depleted of dignity and hemoglobin, her raw humility unnerved me; her brazen bravery unsettled me.

And Jesus' response—His breathtaking endearment which He bestowed upon her—stunned me.

"Daughter!"

She was dumbfounded! An outcast disdained, now a *daughter!* Breathing deeply of this odd oxygen, her once-orphaned, weary spirit exhaled upon hearing His emancipating, parting words:

"Go in peace."

Peace. Watching this indomitable woman, finally holding her head high after twelve grueling years of shame, I was not sharing her peace. I preferred to obsessively check my outerwear, insuring that I had not bled through; I would rather double-up on feminine protection and avoid such audacious acknowledgements than risk embarrassment or exile.

As I watched this no-longer-helpless, no-longer-hemorrhaging sister slowly stride away, I knew my self-conscious safeguarding had made a liar of the beautiful Man-Who-Heals-Dying-Daughters.

Her desperation had declared her messiness to all clamoring to follow Jesus along the road, and, paradoxically, she had been made clean. I, on the other hand, had mentally performed a hysterectomy of my bloody heart, pretending that its endometrial sloughing had remitted.

I stared outside again at the windy waltz of swirling leaves, their jeweled hues shed from barren boughs. I longed to relinquish like bark and branch, surrendering adornments to autumn's whirlwind. I wanted to join hands with the daughter who had risked it all, and profess in front of everyone.

Everyone.

Because I desperately needed to touch Jesus. But I was terrified. And I was unwilling to confess everything.

Everything.

THIRSTY

For an afternoon in May, it was remarkably hot. Concerned about my newly-potted flowers, their colors splashing around the house like playful children, I stepped outside to water them, drenching the pots in the backyard with cool water as I smiled at their happy hues. Walking to the front, I noticed an old, road-weary van stalled by the road directly across from my house.

A middle-aged woman sat behind the wheel, looking as tired as the van itself, while the passenger, a pregnant, younger version of the driver, appeared equally fatigued. I walked over and invited them inside, enticing them with relief from the stifling heat, but they declined my offer.

"Perhaps some water? May I bring you some water?"

"Yes, water would be fine," they agreed.

Packing an empty pitcher with ice, I filled it with water, allowing the frozen cubes to melt into the clear liquid before filling up a couple of plastic water bottles. I grabbed a pack of peanut-butter crackers for the mother-to-be, and delivered the refreshment to the stranded strangers delayed by their cantankerous van. The older woman was pacing by the street, anxiously smoking a cigarette and talking animatedly on her cellphone. Taking the slippery cylinder, she nodded her appreciation and assured me that help was on the way.

I picked up my empty watering can and held it under the surging faucet, the strong, cold stream spraying and energizing me. As water spilled out from the spout, moistening the dark soil sustaining dramatic purple and red petunias, vivacious pink dianthus, and flamboyant orange marigolds—their chromatic crowns demanding daily downpours—my own thirst stirred, nudging within me a recollection of a Man, alone and weary from His journey, stalled by the road as the sun, straight overhead, beat down on His perspiring body.

Closing my eyes, I imagined Him leaning back in my favorite chair—the one Zach had carefully crafted in his woods class—parched lips chapped on His tired face, juxtaposed against the kaleidoscopic annuals holding hands around my patio . . .

"Give Me a drink."

I pointed to myself, inaudible in my reply, scanning the yard as if someone else might materialize. He smiled. Nodded.

I murmured that our tap water was as unfiltered as our lives. Lives stomping around on common ground. Ground not sacred like the site of Jacob's well. That bottled spring water, which I did not have, would certainly be better.

"Why haven't you asked *Me* for water, Lisa?"

Lowering my eyes, I focused on the grass beneath me, green blades craning sunward, stretching up from rain's unrelenting beggar.

How could I ask this of the Man Who Asks for a Drink, when my yawning desire surely plunged deeper than Sychar's watering hole, buried from recognition as it bored for concealed springs through subterranean striations of fear?

"If you keep drinking the same water, Lisa, you will keep having the same thirst."

I slowly exhaled but maintained my downward gaze. I was tired.

Tired of plodding along this narrow ridge of shame, this painful place of longing, only to draw up a salty drop to wet my tongue.

Drops which had only exaggerated my thirst.

"Go, call your husband and come here."

I raised my head and met His eyes.

"You know only my boys and I live here. I have no husband."

"You have correctly said, 'I have no husband,' for

you have had two husbands, and the man you are dating now is not your husband."

His voice was hushed. Tender.

"He is not your husband, Lisa."

The sentence suspended my mind's rotation, halting my racing thoughts—their heady implications dripping down into my shriveled spirit. Their message echoing repeatedly in my heart.

When I had met the man who was not my husband, my maternal heart had been howling for a dad-like hero for Zach.

For Sam.

And arid, cracked plots still remained on the inner landscape of my heart, where my thirst for desirability was still slaked through a glass of masculine desire— the elixir for my loneliness.

The tonic to quench my craving to be sought after.

To belong.

But the saltwater of sex had nauseated me with shame, my soul wailing that this was not the true me. It had become the substitute for the clear, revitalizing water the relationship had never offered.

For over two years I had been treading water in an ocean, swimming alone toward a shoreline of luring light, afraid to tell my friends on the beach I was drowning. Afraid to fight the undertow which dragged me back to the dull, lifeless depths each time I tried to step ashore. The rope I had used to draw up the brackish bucket became the very cord which yanked me back under into a disgraceful, delusional darkness.

It had become a flimsy shoestring tying the relationship together.

But during those cyclical, disorienting waves, the Man Who Asks for a Drink had come, shimmering and wooing, and had whispered to me,

"I want *all* of you, Lisa."

And in this evocative image, I had danced without contours, uninhibited in His multi-colored wind.

I had desperately wanted to be that woman, free and radiant. I had wanted it more than the fleeting security of a male embrace.

Of numb declarations of love.

But like a carnival balloon artist, I had silently—secretly—twisted an unholy sexual bond into a mandate for marriage. I had—like a warped theologian—animated the law. And deadened my soul.

Quietly He waited through my pondering pause before softly responding to my silence.

"You gulp and gag in this saline sea, its briny offerings dehydrating you more and more. Let Me pull you out, and set you in a lush, green field—a place constantly watered by My Spirit. A place where you can worship me in truth. You are My delight and My desire. And I Who speak to you, I Am your Desire . . ."

The back door opened. Zach and Sam came out, mumbling something about food and being hungry. When I turned around, the Man Who Asks for a Drink was gone; my favorite chair was empty. I left my watering pot and followed the boys inside. Peeking out the front window, I noticed the van was gone, too.

As I prepared a snack for my sons, I thought about this rescue. A rescue which required me to reach up for another rope. A life-giving rope being thrown to me in this roller-coastering sea.

A rope to grip.

To trust.

To pull me to quiet, fresh waters.

Waters to sprinkle my heart clean from guilt.

Waters to wash my body in its purity.

And I thought about the unsuspecting woman Jesus had surprised at the well. My Samaritan sister, she had left her heavy, clay crocks and headed unencumbered into the city to tell the men about the Man at Jacob's well. The Man Who told her all that she had done. She no longer cared about their judgments.

About the whispering, disdainful women she might encounter along the way.

About hiding in the isolating heat.

She had encountered the Man Who Asks for a Drink, and nothing else mattered.

I was the woman at the well, measuring my entire life—my entire worth, my "all that I had done"—by the sin that had repeatedly marked my life: I did not love myself well. My prideful pretending. My immobilizing embarrassment. I no longer had to heave these heavy, clay crocks.

I had encountered the Man Who Asks for a Drink, and nothing else mattered.

Bidding my last good-bye to the man who was not my husband, I headed unencumbered toward His luring light. Toward that white, sandy beach—a nude beach, of sorts—where my friends were. Awkwardly, I undressed my soul before them, revealing to them the truth about the relationship.

As I exposed my pale skin—stranger to full sun—I was astonished by the gorgeous grace of their loving acceptance. Their unhesitating forgiveness. A grace that replaced my self-loathing with a self-embrace.

It was a paradox, really. No longer inhibited by my fearful, furtive façade, I could sincerely enfold my beautiful friends.

I could passionately embrace the Man Who quenches thirst.

And I understood what the Sycharian gal had grasped:

Confession is the Emancipation Proclamation of our souls.

To the courageous who speak and to the blessed who listen, nudity inspires nudity.

Authenticity pours in like a summer monsoon, saturating the parched spirit, pooling in the dry fissures of the soul.

I remembered her again as morning blue and boisterous birds greeted me. Flipping to her story which John had shared, I wondered if she had ever given Jesus the drink He had requested. John did not tell us. But John did reveal Jesus' eagerness to tell this seeking, love-starved woman that He was the Messiah.

Discarded by five husbands—and settling for a vow-less arrangement with another—she was the first person to whom Jesus explicitly disclosed His marvelous identity. Ironically, his own thirst and hunger seemed to have been satisfied by His incredible encounter with and exposé to her.

Her.

I savored the connection I felt with her, confident that she would have understood the profounder implication of Jesus' words He had spoken while suspended agonizingly from the cross:

"I thirst."

I stood up and stretched, noticing my flowers outside. They were thirsty again.

It was time to water my colorful collection of glory.

BUCK NAKED

I sat down in her sunny office, a comfortable corner room with as much window as wall. Windows which allowed me to peek out at the vegetable garden flaunting itself like an accomplice in her backyard, summoning me to throw back the heavy curtains—musty and opaque—in the corner of my heart.

It was the third time we had met. Safe and straightforward, she was. Like sitting under Granny's front porch during a splendid summer storm, she had felt like home. But even though I had trusted her with the guidance of my spirit, a nervous reluctance had tagged along with me. A hesitancy to hold her hand as I unlocked this clandestine chamber of my past.

I was fearful of her reaction. I was frightened of losing her liking. I felt as if I had been dragged to the center of the court, clutching the bed sheet around my neck. It had seemed that all the little Pharisees, marching madly in my mind, had shoved me in front of this gentle lady—recounting all the dirty details, scanning the ground for stones.

Stones aimed to keep me crouched and cringing, squinting speechless at the light.

But speak, I knew I must.

I knew I must expose the sonogram of my secret story and give birth to it with words:

Words about an early marriage, college diplomas followed by loveless vows. Vows of hollow recitations hollowing my hungry heart. A heart succumbing to hushed, shadowy passion.

Words about a crucifixion, me, hung between a loyalty to family and a longing for my own.

Me, hung with branded "A" displayed, as the silent innocent was killed.

Killed to spare my family the humiliation the darker skin would have delivered.

Killed to spare the despair my family would have borne.

Killed to cover up the sin which had conceived.

Words about another marriage, obligatory vows protecting an unplanned pregnancy. Vows of determined desperation followed by years of faithful fidelity and faithless fear, nailed to rough planks of harsh abuse—torn between my deserved destiny and my daring desire to break free.

Torn until my dying spirit gasped that it was finished.

Words about a crucifixion, me, sacrificed, beauty laid down for fleeting transcendence, dignity robbed by men.

By me.

Until, half-dead, I had collapsed into the ready arms of Love.

And as I spoke these words to her, her heart stooped low to listen. Her silent tenderness silenced the convicting voyeurs in my head. One by one they marched away, muted as they disappeared. Softly, she had assured me that I was lovely.

That I was loved.

Beautifully broken.

Naked and no longer draped, no longer clasping cover, I considered the gawking crowd being taught by Jesus when the adulterous woman, alone and terrified, was dragged before Him. The stunned crowd, witnessing this sensational scene, had blurred and faded into the background when Jesus had begun speaking to her.

To me.

Truth had set her free.

But, illogically, her full liberation was experienced through everyone else knowing the truth, too. Liberated, because no one—*no one*—not even the cruelest inner accuser or the most condescending in the crowd—had the power to condemn.

She had encountered the face of Christ, the countenance of His complete forgiveness.

I, too, had seen His face. I had seen His countenance in the eyes of this gracious woman who had not condemned me. This woman who had bid me to go.

To go and love Him well.

To love me well.

As I left her light-drenched office, a flirtatious breeze enveloped me like the scandalous grace that had stripped me of my shame. Grace that had clothed me, not in threadbare bedsheets, but in a stunning, white wedding gown.

And now I could face the crowd.

I was free.

This desire to appear what we are not
—artificiality—is one curse that will drop away
the moment we surrender ourselves to His meekness.
Then we will not care what people think
so long as God is pleased . . .
He offers the rest of meekness,
the blessed relief that comes when we accept ourselves
for what we are and cease to pretend.

A.W. Tozer,
The Pursuit of God

Scars and Scabs

SCARS AND SCABS

The owner of the boutique—distracted by her animated conversation with a customer over recent travels to Europe and their shared interest in a Scottish artist—glanced indifferently at us when we entered. Wonderful weather had welcomed Taylor and me to explore the chic shops just a block from my home. Unconcerned about his appearance, Taylor—his thick, black hair unruly, his torn tee shirt and stained shorts unsightly— brashly browsed through the shop while the shopkeeper ignored us.

He commented on various displays, making exaggerated motions while his bared arms begged for attention. Silently I scanned his skin, a canvas harshly splattered with shades of despair and disquiet.

What ruthless tormentor had coerced the blade and slashed across his innocence?

What antagonist had moved anxiety's fingers to pick raw against his tenderness?

Had demons, divorce, disorders, and drugs displaced the

unsullied spirit of the boy who had once sat captive by my side, spellbound by countless books?

Abruptly, Taylor had headed for the door. As we exited, I smirked when I caught the woman's relieved expression. Soothed by the fresh, warm air, I deliberately stepped closer to Taylor, willing the shoulder-to-shoulder body language to convey to any onlooker,

"Yes! He is MY son!"

It was almost amusing. Neurosis, garbed like a happy, homeless vagrant, had strolled down Main Street, and no one appeared to recognize him. No one lingered too long in their looking—perhaps it was too uncomfortable.

Too familiar.

His exposed wounds—some fading, some fresh, some oozing, some obscure, testifying to mistakes and to miseries—belonged to the son I would never dispossess. Never wish to substitute with another.

And I had wondered.

What if the epidermal of my heart could parade down the avenue, like a nude pedestrian displaying her scars from the gashes perpetrated by others, scabs from self-derogation?

Could I so brazenly saunter down sidewalks, risking the uneasy avoidance I might encounter on the street?

When we had arrived home, I suggested to Taylor that he and his brothers and I plan our annual summer waterpark adventure. Taylor immediately declined the offer. Puzzled, I pressed him for a reason.

Removing his shirt, he showed me his chest and stomach. I halted the gasp which sprang for voice as I hastily surveyed the scarlet sores that covered him.

The sight jarred me.

In that timeless, momentary pause, I longed to escape and weep, or simply pretend it was trivial and inconspicuous. Instead I had assured him that the opinions of others were petty. That sunshine and waterslides were good medicine. That soon his skin would be as good as new.

"Just keep your tee-shirt on," I coaxed.

He declined again.

"It is not that I care what others think, Mom. I just don't want to make anyone else there ill-at-ease." Taylor explained. "I know it will get better, that it won't always look this way. But honestly, Mom, I hope it never completely fades, that some scars always remain. They remind me of my struggles. They are a part of me."

Quietly I nodded. I told him that I understood. I reassured him that I wanted him to join our hot-weather ritual simply because I enjoyed him being with us.

Taylor went outside to smoke a cigarette. I stood looking out the window, paralyzed on the holy ground which held me up. Taylor—with all his blatant flaws—was authentic. I was the poser. I desired a smooth, spotless complexion. A mirror that was easy—for me, for others—to stare into.

But without the scars and scabs, how does my life prove that healing has occurred? Without the bleeding, picked places, how can I shout out my desperate need for grace?

Without allowing others to peer at my own battle wounds, I become the tormentor who coerces the blade, the antagonist who manipulates their harm.

My phony perfection robs them of hope.

Was it not the scars seen by the disciples on Jesus' resurrected body that had identified Him? That had offered His disciples immeasurable hope?

I watched Taylor through the blinds, nervously smoking and gesturing as he talked on his cell phone. Though he could not hear me, I spoke softly to him.

To me.

"I don't either, Taylor. I don't want my scars and scabs to disappear completely, either. They are a part of me just as you are a part of me. I love you, my precious, pock-marked Taylor. I love all of you."

Bless the Lord, O my soul,
and forget none of His benefits!

Psalm 103:2 NASB

Scriptural References
Matthew 6:9–15
1 Thessalonians 5:18
Psalm 145:15–16

MOVEMENT EIGHT

Benefits

BENEFITS

I watched her as I was waiting in line to have my groceries scanned. Unlike the other check-out clerks with peppy smiles, her uncombed hair and fatigued face had seemed an extension of the tattered edges of her matching tee shirt.

Sensing an inexplicable connection with this stranger, I had placed fruit and vulnerability before her as I inquired about her day and glanced at her nametag. Smiling at her while slowly arranging the bags in my shopping cart, I spoke her name.

"Angie."

And as if magic fairy dust had been sprinkled over her tired eyes, she began to talk to me, revealing a page of her story which explained why her perky grin and sharp appearance were missing.

Angie had a young son. A young son who did not know his father. A young son who slept in their only bed while Angie slept, exhausted, on the uncomfortable couch. A young son with young-son needs, like clothes and nutritious food. Food difficult to afford. Angie was hoping her out-of-town boyfriend would move in with them soon to help with expenses. With groceries.

I told Angie I was sorry her life was so difficult. Told her I understood the challenges of feeding sons. Of being an all-alone mom. Of not having an extra bed for one of my own sons who was sleeping on the couch.

Handing me my receipt, she stared skeptically at me before turning wearily to the next customer. As I walked out of the grocery store, I was overwhelmed with gratitude for the honor of listening to Angie, for the contents of the plastic bags I unloaded into my trunk. But I wondered how Angie might have responded to me a few weeks earlier, when I had used, for the last time, my food benefits card.

The card of ill-repute.

The card which had presented to me, too often, a haunting humiliation. A plaguing disgrace.

Never would I have had pictured myself as a card-carrying member of this stigmatized class. Me, a woman who had been religiously raised with the axiom that God only helps those who help themselves.

Never would I have dreamed the boys' father would reside in a homeless shelter, incapable of fulfilling his financial obligations of support to his three sons, all of whom were completely dependent upon me.

When I had applied for assistance, hungry boys and bills

had superseded my shame. But the heartfelt thanksgiving I experienced each time I glanced at the simple staples in my cabinets or offered my sons a piece of vibrantly colored fruit, rarely eclipsed my deep dread of handing the thin, plastic card to a cashier. Seldom did my abundant appreciation eliminate my cringing fear that the person behind me would scornfully notice the ignominious card—though it looked like any other credit card.

I had felt like a breathing, moving millstone. A deadweight. Clicking my shoes together and repeating an affirming mantra could not prevent the doors of job opportunity from slamming shut in my face. Could not prevail over my undeniable proofs of burden.

Perhaps I had always seen myself as a burden, constantly considering the needs of others while unconsciously ignoring my own. Always offering up cookies or a card, as if to alleviate the nuisance of my company. As if to earn the companionship of another.

And here I was—frustrated by God's irony—my circumstances validating my relentless perception. Thwarted from earning my keep, I had felt like a loathsome load on humanity, undeserving of God's help. After all, it had appeared I could not even help myself.

I was like a frustrated toddler, trying to wiggle free from the Father's grip, impatient for independence and eager to prove my worth.

But it was He Who proved my worth.

Sitting outside one brilliantly blue-skied morning, I was savoring the serenity of the sweet disharmony of songbirds when God interrupted their refrain.

"I am well pleased with you, Lisa."

It jolted me. It was so unexpected. So counterintuitive to any message I could have contrived on my own.

Well pleased?

With me?

Me? A failure on welfare?

I had little time, however, to consider the divine declaration before my grumpy, retired neighbor appeared, pointing her finger at me as she accused Sam of stealing a few of the miniature American flags which a realtor had poked in all the neighborhood yards for the Fourth of July.

Wincing inwardly as God's lyrical words were snatched up by her indictment, I soon learned that Sam had indeed taken five flags to sword fight with a friend.

Well pleased?

I did not believe it.

Until I heard His voice again.

At the podiatrist.

Zach had been suffering with recurring ingrown toenails, and another toe had become infected. Sitting restlessly in the examination room with Zach, I was silently berating myself for my inability to get a job. Punching myself for not punching a clock. As the podiatrist stepped in to assess Zach's big toe, God—with His odd wit and random timing—countered my sabotaging self-talk.

"What you are doing is very noble, Lisa."

Noble?

Careful to hide any hint of psychosis, I had half-expected the podiatrist to quizzically repeat the word out loud before discussing the removal of the toenail.

Noble.

Noble was a gracious word.

A word that tilted up the chin and looked straight into the eyes.

A word that had never been spotted on my list of self-describing adjectives.

The word spilled over me, quieting all the denigrating voices like drowsy peace. Was it really possible that He was well pleased and considered me noble?

What if it was *not* my shortcomings that had placed me on this path of privation?

What if—as I was sprinting short-winded through the responsibilities of a son with juvenile diabetes and another with juvenile delinquency, never believing I was fast enough, never clearing the high hurdles—God simply wanted to be my Enough?

What if my poverty had placed me on a career trajectory of blessedness, a salaried position in the kingdom of God?

What if God was bestowing on me a hushed humility instead of the condemning humiliation I was lugging?

What if the disgraceful card was actually a Grace card?

As a new toenail gradually grew on Zach's big toe, a fresh protection of trust slowly spread over my heart. Trust in a God Who did not find me the least bit burdensome. A God Who did not expect me to merit His support of the fatherless and the husbandless.

A God Whom King David had praised for opening up His hand and providing meals to all.

All.

Including Angie and her son.

Angie. I had hunted for her many times among the monochromatic-clad clerks, though I never saw Angie again.

But I have seen myself.

I have seen myself through occasional sightings of mothers slipping the covert card to the cashier, treating their child to a sweet indulgence, swapped for an innocent smile. A smile not shared by all when confronted with such a transaction.

Such a transaction should be restricted to generic peanut butter and bags of beans and white rice, I had heard. And I wondered if that was what Jesus meant when He taught us to pray for *our* daily bread, artisanal bread for those who had earned their loaf, day-old bread for those who had not?

How infrequently I had considered the "us" as I absentmindedly recited Jesus' exemplary prayer, my contracted heart murmuring in first person, singular, though my mouth chanted in plural. So focused on my own needs, I had overlooked God's heart. A heart desiring for all to be fed.

All.

Had I assumed a posture of sacrificial willingness during my careless invocation for His kingdom to come, for His will to be done? His will be done—as Paul had succinctly stated—in giving thanks in everything, including our fast-forwarding constant consumption of double-shot cappuccinos and hastily grabbed happy-meals.

Will our incalculable debt of gratitude be forgiven when we rant mercilessly against the free-loading debtors, even as we casually, constantly, take advantage of the unceasing benefits of the ultimate, only, Welfare Provider, Him from Whom All Blessings Flow?

All blessings.

All benefits.

To those granted the mercy of employment

To those dependent upon their mercy.

And to me.

An embarrassing card had told me I could not pay for my own groceries. The Psalms declare that no one can.

That the eyes of all look to God Who gives to all—*all*—their food at the right time.

Perhaps we are all card-carrying dependents, holding in our pockets the beautiful stigma of our utter neediness for His unqualified benefits.

Perhaps, it seems, God always helps those who cannot help themselves.

A closed-up heart can never relax,
never allow you to enjoy another,
to play, to relish the unguarded moment of surprise . . .
Our hearts depend on this Saving Stranger
coming to us and stretching our tight, brittle hearts.

Lonni Pratt and Father Homan,
Radical Hospitality

Scriptural References
Luke 10:25–37

Innkeepers and Robbers

INNKEEPERS AND ROBBERS

My raspy voice introduced me to the morning, my raw throat a reminder of yesterday's rant, an ugly tirade haunting me like a hideous ghoul. An apparition would have been more warmly welcomed than the actuality that had greeted me like the shrill alarm of shame. An alarm without a convenient snooze button to swiftly slam, postponing my awakening.

The day before—possessed by some inexplicable, cleaning caprice—I had begun a maniacal campaign, beginning with long-neglected blinds, brandishing a soapy rag with the frenzied scrubbing of a martyr. Soon my laid-down life was sprawled on the floor, wiping grimy baseboards and sweating as if I was kneeling in Gethsemane, half-believing my cause a self-effacing sacrifice.

With each scouring triumph over the dirty enemy, I became keenly conscious of Sam, sitting sanguinely before the screen, his perky pecking of the keyboard resounding against my eardrum like the dripping water of fictional torture. By the time my crazed, soil-seeking eyes reached the kitchen cabinets, Sam had become (in my ever-diminishing cognizance) an antisocial adult, dwelling in a gaming cyber-world, refusing to assist his exhausted wife. Refusing to visit his elderly mother.

And my textbook psychological profile had swiftly and deftly pole-vaulted from the running start of passive cognition to the airborne hurling of harsh, hateful words, landing with the aggressive thud on the soft padding of Sam's spirit. All the diabolical adrenaline fueling my hysterical sanitization was unleashed. All my fears and frustrations furiously furled—from a filthy cupboard of my soul—at my son.

My son who had few friends.

My son who escaped his loneliness and anxiety through virtual victories and comrades.

Yet I had slaughtered him on the battlefield of real-life.

Me. The tongue-lashing harridan who had—the day before—tenderly taught a lesson to lovely ladies, using Jesus' famous parable of the Good Samaritan.

Although I had earnestly asked Sam to forgive my ireful outburst, my magnifying mirror on the dawning day reflected the unsightly muck still skulking within my spirit. Torpidly, I pulled out the passage from Luke, staring soberly at the familiar words which had so recently resonated fresh and familiar to my heart.

I read the text—reluctantly—again.

My Sunday-schooled viewpoint had always focused on the heroic foreigner who had tenderly triaged the wounded man, sacrificing strength and sandal soles to mobilize the pitiable patient to the nearest Holiday Inn Express. But my blurry eyes began to focus on the cast of characters I had once thought peripheral:

The brutal bandits, lying in wait for innocent travelers;

The callous clergy, circumventing the contaminated zone;

And the nameless victim, slumping half-conscious off the dusty road.

Cringing, I gawked at the scene of the crime, queasy from his garish gashes and bruised body. A body I now recognized.

Sam.

And the incriminating evidence pointed to me.

I was the ruthless robber.

I was the passing priest.

Subject to double indictment, I had ambushed Sam. By permitting his obsessive computer compulsion, I had averted the gory mess of confrontation and conflict. Passively pretending no one had been mugged, I had kept cadence with the clergy, sidestepping the sprawled soul in front of me, keeping life tidy and sanitized through my avoidance.

Yet yesterday's visceral response to his ubiquitous addiction—which I had sanctioned through my ignoring inertia—had blindsided him with a fistful of welting words, stripping him of his self-worth and leaving him half-dead in the ironic puddle of blood I had attempted to obviate.

Closing my eyes to the morning sun breaking through my dust-free blinds, I imagined myself scooping up Sam and placing him on a cushion of our old quilts piled in the little red wagon, the one I had pulled him in when he was too young to bike with his two older brothers. I could almost feel the hard metal of the handle, cold against my hand, as I envisioned myself hauling Sam—scrunched and sleeping—to a cozy, comfortable inn.

To the inn where the last scene from Jesus' narrative was wrapped up like a cliffhanger finale with no sequel. The curtain closes as the compassionate stranger—bone-tired from a sleepless night of nursing—is saddling up his donkey, mounting the mule with a no-nonsense nod to the waving innkeeper.

The innkeeper—the one smiling in his buttoned vest with polished name-tag—is clasping enough coinage in one hand to cover a couple of months' lodging and is holding in the other hand his promise to care for the anonymous, injured guest until the mysterious foreigner returns.

And Jesus had characteristically concluded with an unspoken question beneath the articulated one:

Will the innkeeper prove to be a good neighbor to the one who was placed in his charge?

Will I?

I called Sam down to my room and asked him to sit beside me on my bed while I read to him the poignant parable.

"I've heard this before, Mom."

"I know, Sam. But I haven't. Not like I heard it today. Today I realized that though I am your closest neighbor, I have not been a good one. I have clobbered you with my cold-heartedness and plundered your precious spirit, just like the robbers in the story. I was also the self-deceived religious hypocrite, pretending that your constant computer games were okay by looking the other way. I have not loved you well, and I am so sorry."

"It's alright, Mom."

"No, Sam. It is not. I need your forgiveness. I love you."

I hugged Sam before he slipped out of my room, and I glanced once more at the Scriptures before me. Backtracking to the beginning of the passage, I considered the always-right attorney who had questioned Jesus about eternal life. He was the slick lawyer who had the correct answers, playing by—or, at least, with—the rules.

Had he silently applauded the priest and Levite for adhering to the law and remaining clean?

Had he justified the actions of the murderous marauders, the survival specialists who preyed on those who should have been better protected and prepared?

"Love God, and love your neighbor as yourself," he had arrogantly responded, before adroitly asking Jesus to identify his neighbor.

If he had intellectually assented to the imperative of loving his neighbor and had correctly classified the Samaritan as the target of his love, had he logically deduced which character he had played in the parable?

Had he momentarily found himself at a loss for words, staring incredulously into the eyes of Life as he realized the repercussions of his reasoning?

Had I?

Emptying my hands of Bible and pen, I bent my head and confessed.

I confessed that I was the desperate, broken woman—half-hidden off the trafficked highway, smudged with muck and scarlet, my hoarse voice barely audible—crying out to the approaching Man Who knelt by my side. Lifting up my face, He poured His healing oil and cleansing wine on my needy, helpless heart.

The burnished blinds and buffed baseboards camouflaging my bruised and battered soul removed, He gently lifted me from the dirty ground and delicately lowered me into the little red wagon beside Sam.

Momentarily at a loss for words, I stared incredulously into the eyes of Life, longing to love this Mysterious Stranger with all of my being.

Yearning to shamelessly love myself like this Saving Samaritan loves me.

Desiring to love my neighbors with equal passion.

Especially those who live closest to me.

In this little inn called home.

In some mysterious way,
divine forgiveness depends on us.

Philip Yancey,
What's So Amazing about Grace?

Scriptural References
Matthew 15:21-28
Mark 7:24-30
Philippians 3:10
Matthew 5:6-11
Luke 6:27-28, 35
Revelations 20-21
1 Kings 18:44
Luke 14:27
Matthew 10:38-39
Psalm 37:28

MOVEMENT TEN

I Dated a Thug

PERSISTENT PARIAHS

I glanced up just as he was running across the parking lot, arms flinging formlessly as he raced towards me looking more like my playground-loving boy than my son who was a fresh fifteen. I had been waiting in my car when I spotted his carefree oblivion galloping out of Wal-Mart. Stunned by the holiness of the moment, my heart and face met in a reflexive smile as I savored the sacred seconds before Sam reached me, achingly aware his childlike abandon would too soon be archived by fast-ticking time.

Certainly I had not been leaping lightheartedly lately. My grin had slipped off my face searching for my inner carefree, capering kid who had skipped gloriously down graveled, childhood roads with sun-browned legs lifting high and happy. Injustice had shooed away my insouciant spirit like an unwelcome waif.

For nine months, my sons and I had been stalked, harassed, and threatened by the man I had wished I had never met. His dark e-mails and disturbing texts. His demented stalking. Changing locks and contact information offered little relief from too many beer bottles shattered in our yard and on our driveway, which he had driven by countless times as he honked obnoxiously.

My sons and I had endured his creepy, assailing abuse—never retaliating, never communicating with him. We had only employed the legal avenues urged upon us by the police. By the stalking specialist. By the detective. By the courts.

And I had cried.

Cried for mercy.

Cried for help.

Cried for this demonic presence which had so cruelly tormented our lives to be cast out.

But the expected exorcism had eluded me; instead, betrayal barged in unexpected, stomping on my soul with lies. Ludicrous lies believed by a trusted disciple who had turned his back on me. Perjurious lies spoken under oath against me to an unjust judge— apathetic to truth—gaveling callously upon my innocence.

Staggering in the aftermath, confused, and cleaving to ancient psalms, I had wondered.

Wondered if God had ignored my pleas.

Ignored me.

Wondered if the crying-out-loud Canaanite woman had felt the same when Jesus had ignored her screaming solicitations to heal her demon-tormented daughter.

His disciples—known for pushing pushy parents away—had

turned their backs on this wailing, mulish mom. Irritated by this tenacious Greek woman, they had begged Jesus to get rid of her.

Not deterred by the eye-rolling of twelve annoyed men—not dissuaded by Jesus' ostensible reluctance—she did not back off. She moved in even closer, throwing herself down on the rough ground holding Jesus' feet, begging incessantly, desperately, for Jesus to help her pitiful child, brutally tortured by an evil spirit.

Yet Jesus—skin-wrapped, Compassionate Jesus, Who had healed dying daughters and leprous Samaritans—had snubbed her. Compared her to a dog. A dog not entitled to table food.

And in her stunning, resource-void, fierce maternal love—fiercer than any cruel demon dwelling within her daughter, unfairly altering the course of their lives, lives no longer filled with girlish giggles—she did not care. Though onlookers cringed uncomfortably at her shameless, primitive humility, she did not care.

Hope had stepped onto her turf.

Option-less, she would wait and watch and wait and watch underneath the table, starvation alerting her to any crumb which fell, knowing that even scraps which had fallen from the Master's table had touched the hands of Hope.

Gazing at the groveling Gentile, her remarkable rebuttal courageously uttered, Jesus was impressed.

I was impressed.

And reminded.

Reminded that when fellow followers have wished me away, when I believed I was more like a dog who had dated a thug than a daughter embraced by her Father—when even God seemed to have turned away as I lay prone, fingernails dug around nail-printed feet while others skipped easily ahead—I must tenaciously grate and grip like this persistent pariah morphing Jacobian, refusing to give up, refusing to let go, until the blessing comes.

And the blessing did come to this God-recognizing foreigner. The destructive demon was evicted. Smiles returned to face and heart as Jesus pronounced the most melodic blessing—so marvelous that even his exasperated apostles, known often for their little faith, must have been envious.

Seeing Sam, my boy-man, wild wind sprinting on holy ground, my wondering soul swelled. He tagged the car and threw open the door, panting pink and breathless. My eyes lingered over him, misting, a fierce love overtaking my heart.

And I knew.

I knew God's eyes misted over when He watched me and my sons, stumbling and slogging on gritty roads, His heart distended with indescribable affection for us.

He had invited me—though infinitesimally—into the suffering of His Son, innocent and guilty, obedient and betrayed.

He had bid me into the blessing: morsels of pain and hurt

nourishing dependent humility and uncanny compassion.

Into the prophet's rejoicing reward: to be insulted with evil lies spoken against me.

Into His kingdom's conquering tactics: to pray for, love, and forgive my enemies.

Yes, the floor is hard. The hunger is harder. But I will wait and watch and wait and watch, sprawled expectant underneath His table—residing in and anticipating the blessing—even while others are dining on delicacies.

Because I long to hear Him exclaim the same melodic blessing as He had declared to the resolute Canaanite woman:

"Woman! Your faith is great!"

JUST POINTERS

He walked through the back door after his evening shift at the nursing home looking as tired as the baggy, purple scrubs hanging off his thin frame. But fatigue was not Zach's only companion when he stepped inside our kitchen; a disturbed demeanor had accompanied him as he shuffled past an awaiting dinner and plopped down on the couch across from Sam.

"I really don't know where to start, Mom."

The noticed nuance in his usual, quiet tone prompted me to immediately turn off the television, its empty noise now an intruder.

"Do you remember Dan?"

Although I had never met Dan, Zach had spoken frequently of him. But as Zach slowly disclosed the cause of his disconcertion, he revealed another co-worker, a young gal married to a physically abusive man. Too often her purple scrubs matched the evidence she wore. Dan would sometimes give her a ride when they both worked the early morning shift. A ride he had attempted on this particular morning when the sadistic spouse had directed his violence toward Dan, crashing through Dan's car window.

"Dan shot him."

Three syllables flatly spoken resounded in our living room, as if the gunfire from the morning had finally reached our home. Hesitantly, fearful of the answer, I asked if the man was killed.

Zach nodded his head, half-convincing himself of this surreal reality, an actuality no mother wants brushing against her son.

Pulling up Dan's picture, Zach handed me his phone, describing Dan as the sweetest guy anyone could meet. Staring at his photo, I believed him. Dan looked as young and harmless as Zach, yet Dan had been booked for homicide.

Sam and I sat in silence, the only voice competent to speak into this unsettling moment. Zach rose, and I stood up to hug him. As I held him, a primeval wail welled up inside my soul, silenced by the silent room reminding me to hush.

A hush which haunted me the following few days. Days when prayers were mostly posture—prone and wordless, spirit grieving, Spirit mediating—as I wept for this man-just-shy-of-boy who had defended the defenseless.

Defended his own breath.

This bullet had grazed too close to my heart, knowing how Zach had wanted to champion me. Knowing how justice is a moving target, like a rigged carnival game where only a lucky few get the prize. And I had doubted Dan would be among those fortuitous few.

But he was.

Dan was released, freed from the charges. Innocent. They had found he had assisted with domestic violence and protected his own life.

I was almost asleep when Zach had shared with me the news of Dan's liberation, and my bedroom exhaled with our relief. Our joy. But after Zach walked upstairs for bed, I sobbed.

Sobbed in gratitude for truth's triumph.

Sobbed for the too-young widow, her emancipation blurred by shock.

Sobbed for Dan, recovering from the nightmare that would certainly try to name him.

Sobbed for the man controlled by an evil which had ended his life.

And I sobbed for my son, Zach, closer now to an adult than the teenager who had already known injustice—stepping deeper into a world which appeared unsafe, unjust, his quiet anger tempered temporarily by an uncommon signpost.

A signpost pointing to a time when Justice will come completely—not from my frantic filing of Judicial Complaints.

Not from undue rulings from a judge's bench.

No. Though His Light and Love—through us—are gradually dispelling this present darkness, Justice will finally and fully arrive on a great white throne, obliterating, once and for all, evil.

And in faith, we will wait and watch . . .

FAIRYTALES
OF FORGIVENESS

My knees wobbled as I listened in disbelief to the detective's long-awaited words streaming through my phone.

"Lisa, I just had the pleasure of handcuffing and arresting him at work. He is in jail."

Though the detective had been the strongest advocate for my stalking case, she had not expected to book the malicious man just days after his malevolent intentions had culminated right in my own front yard . . .

> After picking up Sam at the end of his shift at Dairy Queen, we had grabbed a pizza, its warm, cheesy aroma intensifying our hunger as we headed home to share the pie with Zach for a relaxing Valentine's Day evening.
>
> At least, for what we had expected to be a relaxing night.
>
> Piling several slices on their plates, my sons had gone upstairs to their rooms as I had devoured a few

pieces while watching *Dateline,* not ever imagining that in mere minutes my own reality would resemble a potential episode for the show.

Ignoring the intensifying sounds of sirens—a sound quite common on our busy street—I was unconcerned when an ambulance pulled up across the street before stopping at the top of the hill. Unconcerned, until two police cars whipped in quickly behind the ambulance.

Peeking through the blinds, I watched as two officers with assault rifles jumped out of their squad cars, and another policeman shone a spotlight toward our home.

Within seconds, more police vehicles arrived, the commotion drew Zach downstairs, and I nervously informed him the officers were carrying assault rifles. While Zach urged me to stay away from the window, Sam entered the living room, boldly declaring he would step outside to determine the cause of the disturbance, which by this time had escalated to numerous cop cars, a helicopter, and a traffic barricade.

Sam, gallantly portraying the man of the house and ignoring my plea to stay inside, stepped out on the front porch.

Only two words escaped his mouth.

"Hey, guys . . ."

Horrified, I window-watched the surreal scene speedily playing out in the street. Sam was ordered to lie face-down in the road as swat specialists surrounded him with their firearms.

Reflexively I sprinted out the front door, screaming hysterically, only to be promptly greeted by a curt command.

"Put your hands up. Do you have any weapons on you?"

My arms flew up as I shook my head in wide-eyed terror, assuring them I had no guns, begging them to tell me what was going on. Looking back at Sam, I was immediately escorted to the ambulance filled with waiting EMTs. EMTs who informed me a 9-1-1 call had been made by a caller identifying himself as "Zach."

A "Zach" providing our address.

A "Zach" stating he had just shot his mother in the chest.

A "Zach" declaring—with the sound of gunshots in the background—that monsters were everywhere, and there would be dead bodies when the police arrived.

However, while I unknowingly waited in the ambulance, shaking uncontrollably, the real Zach had ventured outside with his hands up. After the swat team asked him his name, Zach was sprawled face-down on the driveway, handcuffed and encircled by rifles. As soon as our home was searched—with my permission—Zach, visibly traumatized, soon appeared and reached toward me for a hug.

Within minutes, Sam, who had been handcuffed and placed in the back of a patrol car, was reunited with me and Zach back inside our once-tranquil living room, now swarming with police.

A detective individually interrogated Zach and Sam as I contemplated the volatile conclusion to a day commemorating love. Earlier that morning I had been completely unaware that "swatting" even existed; by night's end, my sons had become the initial suspects in our personalized version of this too-common prank.

But this was no prank.

And we knew exactly who had perpetrated this intentional act of harm against our family on an evening typically celebrated with cut-out hearts and chocolates. An evening which had concluded with a nearby neighbor unexpectedly knocking on our door, bringing with him much-needed news. He had witnessed the creepy culprit—who had been stalking us for nine months—hiding across the street, watching as the harrowing ordeal unfolded.

This good neighbor had also—just a few nights prior to this terrifying night—been awakened at midnight by the same perverted prowler who was seeking assistance with his truck, which had become stuck in a snowbank while he shadowed our home . . .

The relief of his imprisonment was short-lived, however. Although bond was set extremely high, his mother bailed him out of jail, setting my own apprehension extremely high. Setting in motion the slowly grinding mechanisms of prosecutors and public defenders. Of dockets and detectives. Of staring at the blurred horizon, wondering if justice, like Elijah's storm clouds, would rise up and roll our way. Wondering if I would recognize the hand-sized cloud of righteous rain if I spotted it in the distance.

The dangerous storming of our home had felt like attempted murder. A slight tug on a finger-wrapped trigger could have ended the lives of any or all of us.

But it did not.

Forgiving him had seemed as remote an option as a shower during drought. Actually, I had the impression that forgiveness would act as a storm-chaser, shooing away any drops of justice.

But the words of the One Who actually was murdered—brutally and unjustly—ricocheted in my conflicted heart.

Could I take up my cross—the cross, the coarse altar of suffering and forgiveness—while keeping my fingers crossed and my spirit holding its breath, waiting and wishing for reckoning before risking forgiveness?

Could I pray His kingdom come, when the kingdom of heaven looked just like a scandalous king who, with a brushstroke of white-out on his ledger sheet, cancelled the massive, outrageous debt of a self-saving, fortune-squandering, cold-hearted slave?

Could I expect deliverance from evil—deliverance for myself, for my sons, for this world—while ignoring the powerful means of sabotaging the dark forces of wickedness: forgiving the debts of others as Our Father has forgiven my own debts?

Curiously, an answer came as I sat captivated watching the remake of a timeless children's classic, *Cinderella*, perhaps the most powerful parable outside of Scripture. As the movie comes to its beautiful conclusion, Cinderella is standing at the doorway where the Prince is waiting. Waiting to whisk her away to the castle. To a new life. Cinderella turns to her nefarious stepmother who is seething on the stairway. Looking up kindly at the miserable woman, Cinderella softly says to her,

"I forgive you."

Cinderella twirls back to the Prince, grabs his outstretched hand, and happily heads off to the palace.

Tears streamed down my face as I sat among the mommies and little girls who had just enjoyed the show. But for me, it was more than a touching, enjoyable movie remake. It had redefined forgiveness: an invitation to resurrection.

For forgiveness is not a mindless mumbling that the torment did not matter.

Not a "Get out of Jail Free" card, allowing wicked stepmothers to continue abusing their stepchildren.

Not a magic vacuum, sucking away the penetrating pain from our hatefully harmed souls.

Not a forced shove, pushing us back into oppressive, graceless houses.

No. Forgiveness is choosing to live today in a fairytale, replacing wicked curses with blessing, seeking restorative justice over retribution, and residing in the Prince's palace of unconditional, merciful Love.

It is choosing to live in Thy Kingdom Come.

Whatever I had believed the thug owed us, it could never, ever recompense what had already been robbed from the stories of our lives, which, unlike the remake of *Cinderella,* could never be reenacted again.

The debt cannot be repaid.

No amount of groveling apologies or shame-faced confessions. No amount of money or jail time.

The debt cannot be repaid.

If it could, it would not be forgiveness. It would be nothing more than stained-glass restitution, albeit beautiful, or a generous refusal of another's cash-stuffed hand.

No wonder forgiveness was so hard.

It hurts enough to sweat blood.

Enough to spill blood.

I was reminded of this as I was watching another episode of *Dateline*. A church-going husband and father had had a secret ongoing affair with another woman who had grown tired of waiting for him to leave his lovely wife. Instead of divorcing his wife, however, he had opted for the "easy" alternative: murder via a bomb.

But the wife had survived, and, after two years of rehab, had recovered. At the hearing for the sentencing of this father of three, each child—then young adults—had testified, speaking candidly of their hatred for their father, their unwillingness to ever forgive him, and their complete unconcern for his pathetic soul.

As I listened, my heart winced and ached, knowing they had sentenced themselves to prison as well.

And prison was not the place I wanted to sentence my own heart.

For as long as I called the thug a thug, then I would always be in a victim's jailhouse, and he would always be the creepy culprit, unworthy of forgiveness, impervious to transformation, and incapable of moral behavior —thus, irresponsible and unaccountable for his crimes.

So I knelt down and whispered, "Our Father." I stopped,

knowing I was kneeling beside a weakened, lost man in desperate need of my prayers. So I prayed for this man to collide with Truth. After all, it was the only way he could truly be set free, even if he faced the confining consequences of his offenses, which were still being pursued by the county prosecutor.

When the prosecutor called, she was concise and encouraging. Strong case. Solid evidence. Great judge—a woman and a former prosecutor. Pretrial scheduled. Plea possible, but unlikely. Could we schedule a time to meet and discuss the case?

I plugged in date and time on my cellphone, my heart rate accelerating. Yes, I very much wanted the temporary protection and peace-of-mind his incarceration would offer me and my sons. I inhaled deeply as I reminded myself that the judicial system is a wobbly tightrope to confidently walk upon. A severely flawed system that randomly delivered.

My shoulder muscles had tightened before I noticed I had been holding my breath. Slowly, intentionally, I exhaled, releasing the carbon dioxide-dense air from my body. Releasing the unknown outcome into the winds of Grace where the tiny spores of trust could be inhaled by a Self-giving, fortune-lavishing, tender-hearted King Who exhales His Life and Spirit upon us, galvanizing us to forgive.

The psalmist had assured me that God loves—yes, loves—justice. But the raincloud—still approaching from a distance—looked a little different now, holding in its hazy hand the scales of healing justice. Scales which can only be balanced by the Lover of Righteousness and Justice, by the Lover of a man whose image was not merely a mug shot, but God's.

When the detective called again, she wanted to schedule a time to listen to the 9-1-1 tape? It would be very difficult, she warned. She was right. It was.

Difficult to hear someone telling the dispatcher that he—pretending to be my precious son, Zach—had just shot his mom, Lisa, in the chest.

Difficult to realize that the "someone" on the recording sounded like a teenager instead of the man who was hiding across the street, waiting for the soon-to-arrive squad cars and swat teams.

Difficult to grasp that a young stranger would collude with him in this dark deed. A computer-savvy accomplice who left no track or trace.

Difficult to accept that the Felony charge of Terroristic Threat, which hinged heavily upon my ability to recognize his voice on the tape, would probably—save a miracle, such as the mystery abettor coming forward—be dropped in lieu of a plea to the Misdemeanor charge of Stalking.

Difficult to acknowledge that yet another wicked stepmother had been added to the cast of this ongoing nightmare. As if the narrative required another evil antagonist to thicken the plot.

Another enemy to forgive.

And Peter's preface to the parable of the profligate King and the wicked slave resonated deeply within me, the moaning of his honest words ascending from my soul:

"How many times should I forgive, Jesus? Seven?"

Seven. It seemed so enough. So gratuitous.

Until He answered, opening His Accounts Receivable to the long page headed with my name.

It was blank.

Because the kingdom of heaven is like a King. A King Who had always known that our repayment was impossible. A King Who had always known His Prince would pay what we could not.

I thought of Him, the Prince—beaten body bleeding on crude boards, each breath its own agony—excruciatingly gasping the peremptory words,

"Father, forgive them . . ."

Suffering the curse, He had blessed His enemies and prayed for those who persecuted Him. He had loved the ones who owed Him.

He had loved me.

This forgiveness of the man who had plagued us, it was for me as hard as the wood and the spikes which had fastened His hurt to the cross. And those two, primitive planks—they felt like a precarious pathway to resurrection unleashed. But the Prince was standing in the doorway, His arms outstretched. Tentatively, I reached out to grab them, and as I did, they became two splintered slats.

I took them up and followed the Prince Who had paid my debt.

A year in prison or simply probation, both have been mentioned as possible consequences. Jury trial or plea bargain, either could occur.

I will have to wait and watch.

For He is making my faith great.

For a long time I had sought safety and security
among the wise and the clever, hardly aware that the things
of the kingdom were revealed to 'little children'...
Looking at the handicapped men and women I live with ...
they all have suffered from the experience of rejection
or abandonment; they all have been wounded
as they grew up; they all wonder whether they are worthy
of the unconditional love of God, and they all
search for the place where they can safely return ...

Henry Nouwen,
The Return of the Prodigal

Scriptural References
Luke 14: 1-24
John 13:5-10

MOVEMENT ELEVEN

I Want
My Mommy

I WANT MY MOMMY

Only two lap lanes were open in the middle of the pool. Splashing and kicking with their swim instructors beside one of the roped-off lanes was a bevy of toddlers and preschoolers, their happy noise muffling the music to keep the older women on pace in the water aerobics class on the other side of the pool.

I had just begun my pool run in one of the coveted lanes—submerging myself in the restorative water and savoring the sounds of rambunctious life all around me—when the piercing scream of a tot muted the ongoing raucous all around.

"I want my Mooooooooommy! I waaaaaaaaant my Mommy!"

Mommy, however, was walking with her other kids to the bleachers, where most mommies (and a few daddies and grandparents) waited, watching their adorable swim students while keeping their other children away from the pool. This tiny boy had not taken his eyes off Mommy, extending his small arms toward her while relentlessly shrieking his desperate mantra over and over.

At first I was amused, remembering my own sons' phases of

mommy-clinging. His patient instructor appeared completely unbothered by the child's incessant yelping and lack of cooperation. Mommy remained in the bleachers, smiling reassuringly. I intensified the scissor-like motion of my workout, pretending to adopt the same, unaffected attitude of the swim teacher.

But the stubborn, sweet one refused to stop his hysterical pleas for Mommy. I began to telepathically send messages to Mommy, advising her to stand resolute and not cave into the begging of her little manipulator—I mean, her little precious. My covert persuasion worked; Mommy did not budge.

I fantasized about the boy collapsing as he spit out his exhausted vocal cords into the chlorinated, blue liquid surrounding him, his voice floating away like a lovely dream.

But he did not.

As his hoarse harassment echoed through every molecule in the water—and through any remaining oxygen which had not been sucked up by the beloved boy's lungs—everyone else at the pool strangely seemed to evaporate from my peripheral awareness.

Everyone except the aberrant boy still determinedly maintaining his loud cry for Mommy.

Switching to faster intervals, I was sensing that these stormy sound waves from this desperate boy were intended more for me than his Mommy. That the One Who can calm a raging sea had allowed the toddler's tornadic tirade especially for my ears.

For I knew that constantly thrashing about beneath the surface of my soul was an obstinate tot of a girl, her arms flailing upward as her egocentric crescendo squawked out countless completions to her unyielding "I want my . . ."

Loneliness had become a constant tag-along, too often my loudest—yet loyal—companion. The pain which only sleep removed stretched out before me like a cinematic highway in the desert. I wanted provocative dialogue with like-minded theologians. I wanted constant companionship with like-hearted ladies.

And I was tired.

Tired of expending myself on hoped-for friendships, always initiating. Always inviting. Rarely invited.

Invited.

I wondered if there was a more substantial word to buoy a sinking soul. To fill-in-the-blank of the "I want my" equation. I wanted to be invited.

Invited.

Luke's gospel account revealed that it was certainly a weighty word to Jesus, too. A prestigious Pharisee had invited Jesus to join him and his peers—and an oddball guest with dropsy—for a Sabbath supper and seditious scrutiny.

But it was Jesus Who was eyeballing them with more exact examination, their jockeying for the prime places among the religious celebrities at the table. And when Jesus took hold of the most unlikely guest—the one whose body was freakishly distended with fluid, the one Jesus had been sitting behind—and healed this unclean man, their pretentious pecking order was flipped upside down.

After sensitively sending away the miraculously restored guest of honor, Jesus had pointed out to the arrogant, aggressive invitees that they should have put first dibs on the now-vacant, back-row seat.

Then He pointed out to the hoaxing host that he should have invited the poor.

The blind.

The disabled.

The deficient.

The flawed.

The offensive.

The contemptible.

The inferior.

The ineffective.

The insignificant.

The impaired.

The imperfect.

The uncool.

The undesirable.

The unimpressive.

The un-substantive.

The un-needed.

The un-good.

The un-beautiful.

The un-smart.

And the unable to repay.

After all, extending luncheon invitations to those-most-likely-to-reciprocate—friends, brothers, relatives, and rich neighbors—was simply a graceless ticket to a hoped-for exchange.

And if friends, brothers, relatives, and rich neighbors were excluded, the invitation list left little room for anyone.

Anyone except strangers.

And Jesus had already thrown an enormous dinner party for over four thousand starving strangers who had been following Him around for three days. Not only had these impoverished blind, crippled, lame, and mute strangers stuffed themselves at the bottomless bread-and-fish buffet which Jesus had so compassionately provided, they had been healed by Jesus as well. Jesus had expected nothing in return, fully aware that the hungry crowds would never—could never—repay him.

Anyone except ordinary neighbors.

And Jesus had already defined "neighbor." The one we love as we love God and ourselves. The one as despised as a Samaritan. A Samaritan who cared for an abandoned, dying man who needed healing.

Were those smug Sanhedrin and dutiful Pharisees even listening to Jesus? Until Jesus had mentioned the repayment at the resurrection of the righteous, their ears had not seemed to perk up. But at this remark, they had raised their goblets in a toast to themselves:

"Here's to us, the blessed ones who will definitely be eating bread in the kingdom of heaven!"

And in the clinking of their cups, I had recognized my own repetitive, childish demands, my own inward begging to be included among the spiritually agile. My own wiggling into a seat at the popular table. A table which had served up ostentatious excuses and eleventh-hour rejection by those with bigger things to do and better people to do it with.

By those who have no need for yet another invitation.

And I wondered.

Was it in the loneliness—in the place where the shunned and the feckless reside—that the invitation begins its seductive dance, its mysterious movements noticed and needed only by the broken and forgotten? By those who would never decline the slave's solicitation to feast at the Master's table?

Is it not the poor in spirit, the hungry, the thirsty, the persecuted—the true blessed ones—who gratefully accept and enjoy the big dinner set before them?

I remembered when Zach's high school principal had noticed Zach—hidden by average grades and peripheral position—and invited him to apply for a job at his friend's successful company. Thrilled over being hand-picked when he was accustomed to being overlooked, Zach was wooed and wowed by invitation's allure, which eventually had won him the job.

I remembered when a good friend had invited Sam and me to spend a long, summer weekend with her parents at their lovely lake house. It was as if Grace had scurried out into the streets and found unsuspecting us, lavishing us with a well-needed getaway which we could not afford. We were treated and fed like royalty; any offer of payment or reciprocity would have been offensive.

It had seemed too good to be true.

I doubted that any of the religious elite who had shared that Sabbath supper with Jesus had considered His paradoxical parable as too good to be true. To the proud Pharisees and select Sanhedrin, it was inconceivable that unclean outcasts— like the suffering man whose swollen, distorted body was being used to bait Jesus—would be the sought-after guests for a sumptuous party.

And it was even more preposterous that they, the Who's Who of the Always Invited, would never taste of that delectable dinner. A dinner only savored by those whose handicapped hearts had been humbled and healed. By those whose utter broke-ness and brokenness had rescued them from sightless self-sufficiency.

Maybe cliquish, comfortable companionship—like a tiny table within a heavily draped dining room—would have blinded me to my own broke-ness and brokenness. To the crippled condition of the needy and the nobodies.

I recalled my latest search for financial assistance with Sam's diabetes, which led me to find help through a program for the medically handicapped. Their modest offices were tucked in the back of an old building where two unpretentious women worked diligently for disadvantaged kids.

Walking through those unassuming doors—with no means to provide the necessary supplies for the treatment of Sam's medical handicap—and walking out knowing that nothing was expected in return for their priceless provision, I was overwhelmed.

Overwhelmed not merely with gushing gratitude, but by the glaring exposure of my concealed, competitive urges; the ripping away of unfounded, hidden haughtiness; and the penetrating provocation to admit my own disabled and deficient status. A status which ranks me among the invited:

The needy nobodies.

The lonely losers.

The prostituted pariahs.

Yet could I truly step within and beyond the metaphor to seek and summon such strange neighbors to eat around my nicked-up old table, serving them plates piled high with a hearty meal, its heady aroma an irresistible invitation to feast and to belong and to be loved?

For in feeding the least of these, Humility Himself is a guaranteed Guest, seated behind—and mysteriously within—untouchable castaways and contemptible hypocrites, dishing up a deeper healing than that found among the smart and savvy.

I reevaluated my special friend, Richie, who is always singing and shouting loudly to the music streaming from his earbuds as he walks all over the small town where I live. Richie often stops by to use my computer or to ask for a ride. He talks enthusiastically about his favorite world-class wrestlers and the odd jobs he always finds to earn money. Born with fetal alcohol syndrome, Richie would rarely—if ever—appear on someone's guest list or be included in a weekend get-together. I, too, might have shut out Richie, had it not been for the ironic gift of my loneliness.

I considered one of my dearest friends, now restricted to a wheelchair. A wheelchair holding—and belying to the casual observer—an artist, poet, vocalist, pianist, guitarist, and extraordinary cook. Never do I experience such pleasant authenticity as when I am hanging out with her.

I recalled when this amazing woman—who has endured more physical, mental, spiritual, and emotional suffering in her thirty-five years than a thousand lifetimes should ever bear—prepared an over-the-top Vietnamese meal for me and another close friend.

The delectable meat had marinated for three days.

The sweet rice had soaked for twenty-four hours.

Her table was covered with exotic condiments to enhance the delicious feast.

The cooking alone demanded from her a gymnastics performance, as she balanced precipitously on her rolling walker.

I was awestruck. A writer without words. Only the words of Peter surfaced in my heart as I marveled at this sacred communion.

"Lord, do *You* wash *my* feet?"

And in that lowly, leveled posture, my vantage point shifted. And I saw.

I saw it was not primarily the Sams and the Richies and the wheelchair-bound who needed me.

It was I who needed them.

No wonder Jesus had instructed us to invite them to our

bounty-laden, round tables.

I saw a compassionate Papa, His food-smeared apron flapping as He beat down the bushes searching for the feeble and forgotten—as He barged in old buildings with unadorned cubicles and uncelebrated clients—motioning with His oven mitts to come to a mouth-watering feast fixed just for them.

For me.

I had been invited.

Invited.

I returned to the pool the following week. The same little boy arrived shortly after I had slipped into the refreshing water. Letting go of his Mommy's hand, he allowed the swim instructor to hold him before they dipped into the cool, blue Mommy-less world.

I braced myself, waiting for the shrill wailing to begin.

But, astonishingly, it did not.

The happy, little tike was smiling and splashing, content in the arms of his swim instructor.

Relaxing, I noticed that the obstinate tot of a girl within me was no longer thrashing about, either.

And I wondered.

What undulating waves of healing might occur if I completely let go of my childish "I want's" and infantile social preferences, and looked for the lame and the lost?

If I consistently invited the consistently uninvited to my wobbly dining room table, its paint chipping from boys and too many moves, and spread out a bottomless buffet—not for the corporate credentialed and likeliest leaders—but for the least likely to succeed?

At the surface of my soul, a fresh prayer was forming.

"Lord, I want to be an inviter. Help me to notice the unnoticed. I want my unadorned dining room and unstable table to always have an open space for the uncelebrated."

I looked up to the bleachers at Mommy and secretly congratulated her for her unseen—and unheralded—heroic feats of motherhood. I glanced back at the boy, smiling at the small stroke of maturity I had witnessed in him.

In me.

When I stand among the tombstones
of the casualties of my soul, lingering over each inscription,
morning light shoves its way between each marker, gradually
dispelling mourning's mist as the brightness
of the overwhelming graces stream amid
the meager memorials of my story.

Lisa Curry

Scriptural References
Genesis 11:27–Genesis 13:18
Genesis 21:1–5
Matthew 5:3–12

Luke 7:11–15
Ruth 1–4

John 5:1–17

MOVEMENT TWELVE

Little Deaths

CORNFIELDS AND BLACKBIRDS

I heard the back door unexpectedly open. Loud footsteps followed, and I stood frozen in the kitchen, panicked, until Zach's face appeared, beaming at me exuberantly as he announced that the graduating seniors had been released early on their last day of school. Holding his cap and gown folded primly in plastic packaging, his smile as bright as the red he held, he informed me that he and his friends were heading out for a celebratory lunch. Tossing the proof of his fresh freedom on top of the refrigerator, he stepped out the back door, leaving as abruptly as he had arrived.

The kitchen resumed its quiet humming, and I slowly pulled my eyes up.

Up to the shiny, clear wrapper encasing the undeniable verification of his adulthood.

My throat constricted while tears greeted me as surprisingly as Zach's just-a-moment-ago arrival had, and the ancient, maternal moan bellowed bittersweet within my heart, its melodious melancholy interrupted by the ringing of my cellphone.

It was the prosecuting attorney for the felony case against the stalking man.

The swatting charges had to be dropped. The 9-1-1 call—most likely from a throwaway phone—could not be traced. She punctuated her disappointing news with encouraging words about the solidity of the stalking trial before ending the call as rapidly as Zach had exited.

The dining room where I sat fell silent, as if the walls were watching with O-shaped mouths, awkwardly shuddering—as I was—in stunned disbelief.

My affective capacity had hit critical mass.

But in an act of cognitive compassion, my mind reached out to my heart, meandering back years ago when my determined face was moistened not with tears, but with sweat . . .

> Turning northward, the demanding half-mile hill completed, I grimaced and grinned at the upcoming incline. Stretching acre upon acre, edging both sides of the pastoral road, the outstretched arms of browning, crackly cornstalks proudly saluted me as I shortened my stride, their regal posture belying their dwindling tour of duty. As I passed each row, I felt as if these Midwestern soldiers were spurring this out-of-breath private through their ranks, and I welcomed their galvanizing gesture.
>
> I had been learning to look for odd, extended

hands on this faith-forged, map-free, pay-as-you-go adventure. An adventure which had allowed me to share bagels with a friend for breakfast one weekday. A breakfast which had caused me to believe— somewhat apologetically, somewhat guiltily—that I should not be enjoying such a carefree indulgence. It has crossed my mind that I was acting as if I had a munificent husband. But God, aware of my rumination, had promptly interjected,

"You do. I Am."

His simple, silently-sensed sanction had propelled me on this Abram-like journey where I was venturing.

No credit cards.

No career.

No cultural conformity.

No bullet-point plan.

No fast-track formulas.

And I had wondered what peculiar reassurances Abram had encountered on his way to Canaan.

Canaan. The intended destination of Abram's father, Terah, before he pulled off the road at Haran, feeling at home among the green-eyed gods of this Ur-like town. Its pagan darkness had seduced Abram's surviving brother, too; he married his niece and dug in his tent stakes in this god-mongering domain.

But not Abram. Abram unquestionably had heard God call, an untenable call to leave "Your"—the secure and the familiar of family and friends and salary and suburban home—and to set out, at a most unlikely and inconvenient time, toward the undefined land of "I Will."

I, too, had heard the call, standing by my bedroom window one morning—the call beckoning me away from my will—inviting me into to a portable shelter of yet-to-come promises written on an invisible contract of hope.

Inviting me into I Will . . .

Walking back into the kitchen, incredulous at the sprinting, passing years, my pooling eyes peered back up to the shrink-wrapped red. How had we so quickly arrived at this half-happy destination of graduation garb? At this ostensible detour of injustice? I felt as if I had pulled over on the shoulder of this Canaan highway, confounded by the road sign ahead:

"Welcome to I Will!

And directly beside it, a bent and battered marker—distance omitted on the unhelpful green metal—flatly announced the next town:

"I Will."

Too soon, however, I was ironing scarlet solemnity before sitting in a gymnasium swelled with pride and parents. A gymnasium where I held hands with tender, boyish recollections of yo-yos and speed-stacking cups and blue bicycles. Of adolescent angst and faithful friendships.

And as a flock of tasseled caps was fervently flung upward toward an unsuspecting ceiling—and each other—another memory tugged at my tears, as if they needed persuasion . . .

It was me, on another run.

Same route.

Same sunburnt cornfields of withering stalks.

And I was pacing myself up the first eight hundred meters of intensifying effort when, catapulting from the browning relics of a farmer's toil, hundreds upon hundreds of blackbirds sprang skyward from the dying shoots, flying freely into morning's firmament.

Pounding pavement on a rural run, already breathless, I was staggered by a Creator Who had rustled up a magnificent sideshow as He jogged beside me . . .

Rising as the heads-held-high seniors marched out of the gym—rivulets tracing over my makeup—I knew.

I knew I was an aging, wrinkling cornstalk, saluting my Tenderfoot as this particular tour of duty was fading. Letting loose of him as he was hurled—green and nascent—into dawn.

Walking out of that gym, I had felt more like Sarai than Abram, a little more barren than I was before. And as cameras clicked a pic of me and my diploma-bearing son, mysteriously, I felt a bit more beautiful, too.

The next day, Zach had barged through the back door—again— his countenance as elated as it had been a few days prior. Smiling, he was nodding his head, and I did not need to ask him.

"They offered *me* the job, Mom!"

Equally wowed and wistful, I gave him a congratulatory bear hug. He had already landed a full-time, grown-man job. A good job with benefits and educational opportunities. Distracting myself from my too-eager tears, I jokingly remarked that it was fortunate we still had some leftover graduation cake to celebrate his good news. Laughing, he loped upstairs to his room, and I was left standing in the kitchen alone.

Again.

Faint chords of sadness sounded in the silence, until the words which God had spoken to Abram as he scanned the unfamiliar landscape searching for I Will, quieted this mother's low lament.

God had vowed to Abram *and* his offspring the blessing which *He* would accomplish.

Jesus, too, had promised the Blessing, detailing a recognizable topography of Canaan—a land of poverty, mourning, humility, hunger, thirst, mercy, and persecution—where He bid the brave to follow Him.

Where He welcomed weary pilgrims, and directed them to their next stop: I Will.

Where an unobscured kingdom vista was inhabited by His comfort, satisfaction, inheritance, and rewards, all waiting for those wayfarers plodding behind The Followed One.

Standing in the solitude of my kitchen, I suddenly did not feel alone. It seemed I had, like Abram, trekked all around—near Bethel, through Negev, sidetracking in Egyptian betrayals like lovely, lonely Sarai, and backtracking to Negev and to Bethel—until I finally stopped in the Hebron of this moment, lifting my eyes, not northward or southward or eastward or westward, but inward.

For the luxuriant oaks of Mamre, where tent pegs take root and rocks turn to altars, are only discovered within the geography of the heart.

In this meandering, nomadic I Will, dry ditches of truth and hollow halls of justice have provoked a ravenous hunger and thirst for righteousness. Sorrow has tilled the heartland for seeds of comfort, as every teardrop—proceeding from the waterfall of the Weeping God—has irrigated deep furrows of mercy and gentleness.

And I was reminded—on this ascending, switch-backing highway, limned from the rough-hewn beams dragged by the travelers who have gone ahead of me—of another run, more recent, on that hard, half-mile hill . . .

> I was oblivious to the drought-stricken corn crops—
> crepe-papery, rain-robbed russet sheaves atop

panting, parched ground mimicking me—until a precipitous, cool gust rushed across field and face, sounding like thousands of children whispering a bit too conspicuously.

Startled, I looked across the tiered farmland as corn-bearing ghosts, now animated and chatty, were being resurrected by a deep, windy Sigh from the north. I stopped my focused footfalls mid-hill and gasped, sweat stinging my eyes. Stretching my arms like a small girl trying to touch the sun, I worshiped in astounded recognition of my utter, incessant need for His Breath to blow fresh and fierce through me, ever cycling from green to brown, from green to brown . . .

Walking out of the kitchen, I noticed a crumpled, red pile in the spare bedroom. Zach's castoff cap and gown had been clumped in a corner, lifeless, their fleeting purpose fulfilled. Tears were forming.

Again.

And I was keenly aware that, like my cornstalk companions— sometimes saluting, sometimes releasing, and sometimes bearing sweet, golden corn—I would always, *always,* be dependent on the vivifying gales of His Spirit coursing through this aging life of mine.

A jury trial had been scheduled. Zach's first day at his new, manly job was just a short distance away. And three baby birds, nesting in my backyard, had grown far too big for their tiny, straw habitat. Captivated by their gangly, stretching wings, I was assured there would be more unconventional assurances along these winding roads of I Will.

I imagined Abraham again, all tears and laughter when Isaac, squalling and pink, was finally handed to him, and I knew.

I knew that Canaan—regardless of jury verdicts and flyaway sons—was not a wished-for outcome, an exotic location, or emotional homeostasis.

It was the fulfillment of the Promise.

Like Issac, I Will is a Person.

I Will is I Am.

And it seemed I was already home.

Again.

BITTERSWEET SIXTEEN

I had not wanted to go up there.

Not yet.

The game-changing weekend was still brushing against my back, and I was still brushing back tears. Excluded from Sam's Sweet Sixteen celebration, I, a study of split-faced emotion, had watched Sam and Zach pull out of the driveway in Zach's brand-new, black car. Destination: a brothers-only adventure to Worlds of Fun.

It was the first time I had ever been omitted—like an unnecessary word in an exclamatory sentence—from a son's birthday party, and the day had elongated empty and endless, its heaviness constantly bearing down on me, reminding me of Zach's announcement a few weeks earlier that he and his buddy-from-childhood would be getting an apartment. Reminding me that Zach would be moving out of the house the very next day.

But shortly before this amusement park getaway, Zach had arrived home from work, his demeanor as blue as the technician's uniform he was wearing, and had flopped down at the dining room table, his head resting on the worn wood which had held countless plates of home-cooked meals for him.

Watchfully, I knelt down beside him as quiet tears emerged from my Tenderfoot. Resting one hand upon his lean frame as my other hand stroked his thick hair, I had softly asked him what was wrong. He shook his head as if confused by the uninvited emotions that had barged in, catching him off guard.

Fidgeting with his cellphone, he found the thread of texts which his father had sent him. Hollow, disappointing texts sent to my son-no-longer-boy, yet the boy within him was crying out for a father to guide him across the tape as he stretched toward manhood.

Crying out for wise words which only a father can speak.

Barely whispering, I gently inquired,

"What would you want your dad to say to you? What would you love to hear?"

As silence stood between us, I continued to faintly brush his hair with my hand, until his thoughts bravely became words.

"I guess I want him to say 'I'm sorry.' That's it. 'I'm sorry.'"

My breath caught, and in the intensity of this sacred dialogue—in the ferocity of my mother-love—I longed to absorb into my flesh all the disappointment and pain and confusion suspended in this moment.

But I could not.

I could only trust the True Father to walk beside my son-no-longer-boy.

To walk beside me.

To walk beside me as Jesus had walked beside the grieving widow of Nain, weeping behind the pallbearers who were carrying her only son, dead in a dark, airless coffin. The large crowd following Jesus to Nain had converged with the sizeable funeral procession, a wailing commotion heading out of the village's gate. In spite of all the blurring people compressed into this confluence, Jesus had zeroed in on her.

Her, the emptied-of-everything woman-turned-worthless.

Her.

The one Jesus saw.

And as her tears dripped down on the coarse, black fabric of her hopelessness, the heart of Jesus had ached with hers—knowing He would absorb into his flesh all the disappointment and pain and confusion suspended in this moment—as He tenderly spoke to the sad and sonless woman my own unspoken plea to Zach,

"Don't cry."

He had spoken those words to me, too. Over twenty-five years had passed since I had heard them, standing statue-like by shoveled dirt on that overcast and chilly December the twenty-third, waiting by the waiting grave.

Waiting for the wee casket to be lowered into a hole dug smaller than the one dug rough inside of me.

My sweater was the faintest pink, the pink of baby's breath tender against one's cheek. Baby's breath which would never caress my cheek again. My posture had matched my pale, pink skirt, straight and stoic, as I braced my body for the burial of my firstborn, my arms emptied of his warm innocence I had cradled for twenty-two days.

Mama had sewn him a yellow teddy bear, a bear as yellow as the sun that was hiding on that day. Hiding like the yellow bear, which was tucked at Jacob's side. Hiding like death's cold stare, which was concealed within his tiny coffin. But, saying goodbye to my infant son who had never shared my breast or home, I could not hide from my grief.

And neither—with over a quarter of a century having passed— could I hide from my grief with Zach's pending move. For over twenty-five years, life had seemed, in a way, a sequence of little deaths—of losses usually shrugged off with, "It's just life," when, really, it was death.

And I did not want to simply shrug off this little death, this transitional farewell to Zach. For without a proper burial, the blessedness of mourning would be lost, a blessedness only bestowed on those grieve. For without grief, what need was there for comfort?

And comfort came upon my hearing Jesus' beautiful, bewildering salutation to the widow of Nain. Upon my gawking with the curious crowd, staring stupefied when Jesus traipsed right up to the crude, concealing box, and touched it.

Immediately His death-defying exclamation penetrated the sudden inertia.

"Young man, I say to you, arise!"

And the young man did!

The resurrected son-no-longer-dead sat up and spoke!

I sat up, too, thunderstruck like the slack-jawed mourners and the wide-eyed followers of The Resurrection!

Jesus had restored the once-decaying, only son to his mother-no-longer-mourning.

Jesus had cared so much for a despondent, weeping widow that He dramatized the inauguration of His kingdom through her story.

I was reminded of Naomi, another despondent widow, though more ancient than the woman of Nain. Having lost both her sons and husband in a foreign, pagan country, Naomi's loss was more severe.

But when Naomi had returned to her hometown of Bethlehem, she was not quite as barren and desolate as she had perceived and proclaimed; her humble, selfless, and lovely daughter-in-law, Ruth, had faithfully followed her home, devoting herself to Naomi's care.

And after Ruth had married Boaz, she gave birth to their son. But the boy was placed upon *Naomi's* lap, and the women of

Bethlehem laughed and named the boy Obed, because a son had been born to Naomi!

Indeed, mourning had morphed into comfort for these women, and I knew it would for me, too.

———————◆———————

With new confidence, I looked upstairs.

I was ready to go up there.

Slowly and deliberately I ascended each step, certain that the One Who zeroed in on emptied arms and plopped life in unfilled laps was climbing up with me. Opening the door to Zach's old room, I held my breath as I surveyed the vacant, silent space. The walls were void of all the posters from his favorite video games. All the cords and wires and dirty clothes—and even clean clothes—no longer covered the stained carpet. His frumpy bed, once cozy in the corner, had disappeared, too.

Surveying the remaining dust and dirt, which the unrefined sight of eighteen-year old young men are incapable of spotting, I resolved to start scrubbing right away, a surefire distraction from the heavy footfalls of melancholy I heard treading toward me.

I picked up a broken lamp he had left lying on the floor. The boisterous boy-sounds which had once filled this space had been muted, its white noise so deafening I had turned to walk out. But another sound—a sound of words so delicate they were almost imperceptible—stopped me in my tracks.

"Don't cry, Lisa. Don't cry."

But this hushed, holy entreaty was quickly followed by the thud of marching on the stairs. Sam had returned home from his shift at Dairy Queen, and he was eyeing me quizzically, his logical brain attempting to grasp my heart-on-my-sleeve demeanor.

"Mom, Zach will be living fifteen minutes away. It's no big deal!"

Smiling at Sam, I agreed and disagreed.

Sam. His lively energy bounced off the four walls enclosing the abandoned room, and landed right in my lap.

"How was work?" I cheerfully asked him, pulling him in with an affectionate side-hug. Laughing to myself, I had wondered how his analytical mind would respond if I playfully called him Obed.

Instead, I allowed the exclamation of Sam's conversation to penetrate my momentary inertia as my wide-eyed heart gawked at the goodness of Life.

Life.

He had certainly sauntered alongside my boys and me, stepping right up to coffins and barren bedrooms, and had touched what no one else could touch.

And had spoken the words which no one else could speak.

LICENSE

Sitting on the uncomfortable, slatted bench at the DMV, I was unable to concentrate on the book I had carried along to read while I waited for Sam to take his road test. It was his third attempt to pass. His third attempt to toss aside his learner's permit, and get his hands on a real, I-can-drive-without-Mom license. And I had a bit of a slipknot in my stomach as I waited.

When Sam finally appeared around the corner, he was wearing his signature half-smirk, his inner celebration usurping his contrived countenance as he pretended he had failed again. But he had not. Smiles spread out over both of our faces—the kind of smiles which felt as if our faces were constricting our happiness.

After triumphantly pulling away from the parking lot, Sam drove us to Starbucks for a caffeinated toast before dropping me off at home and heading to school.

By himself.

Without me.

I stood on the front porch while he gallantly steered away, his

elation tumbling out of his open car window and dabbing my
tears away. In a mere morning, his brand-new independence
had redefined the ordering of my days. He no longer needed
me to ride with him to and from school, or to ride with him to
and from work.

It felt as if his fresh freedom would not simply redefine my
schedule—it would redefine *me*.

Kneeling by his bedside, without his breezy jubilation to hinder
my crying, I wept loudly, allowing the inviolability of this
moment—of this trail's culmination at an unfamiliar trailhead—
to console me as I mourned and marveled at Sam's new mobility.

And mine.

And I was reminded of the long-lame man, lying immobile by
the pool of Bethesda . . .

> His infirmity had crippled him for almost four
> decades, with no one to lift him into the lottery
> of seldom-stirred waters. The outline of his limp
> body was imprinted on his pallet of resignation and
> misery; it seemed that his poor choices had deposited
> him there among the pitifully sick children and the
> woefully withered elderly.
>
> Among the unsighted beggars and the helpless
> paralyzed.
>
> Among the candidates who were more deserving of
> the pool's sporadic cure.

With Passover in full swing, Jerusalem was congested and chaotic on the day Jesus was taking a Sabbath stroll, striding right past the five colonnades surrounding the sacred site, stepping right past the desperately waiting, and stopping right beside this inert and ignored man. His atrophied limbs, his repulsive sores, his grimy stench—these did not repel Jesus from approaching the repugnant invalid and questioning him with non sequitur.

"Do you wish to get well?"

As perplexing as Jesus' query might have seemed, the man's response was equally puzzling. Rather than averring with a resounding "Yes!" he had instead launched into a victim's spiel.

The crippled man made no passionate plea for healing.

He expressed no radical revelation of faith.

No earnest entreaty to carry him down to the pool for a long-awaited dunk in the mysterious waters.

Yet, in spite of his lame attitude, Jesus had squarely confronted him with a candid command.

"Get up."

"Pick up your pallet."

"Walk."

Immediately—before he could even lift up his foot—he was healed. And without even a "thanks a million" to the One Who had animated his shriveled, useless limbs, the once-incapacitated man picked up his pallet and walked away.

Yet, in spite of the ingratitude, Jesus had searched for the now-ambulatory man. After finding him in the temple, He squarely confronted him with a candid command.

"Do not sin anymore, so that nothing worse happens to you."

Jesus' confounding conversation with this former poolside fixture had come full circle, His ending comment as odd as his original question . . .

Why would an emancipated man choose emaciation again?

I thought of how ridiculous it would be if Sam, proud possessor of a new driver's license, returned to the dreadful DMV, requesting that the helpful clerk hand him back his learner's permit.

But Jesus recognized the man's proclivity for pallet-lounging on the beach, feeling more at home among the diseased and dependent than among those running responsibly away from Bethesda.

Sitting in my grief on the edge of Sam's bed, I recognized my own bent for slouching by the pools of my melancholy. But Jesus was asking me if I wanted to be healed from the losses my finitude was perpetually positing.

He was asking me to grab my pallet.

He was nudging me to move forward.

My pallet had become like the ones my Granny used to make for me as a little girl, old blankets piled thick on the floor where I could nestle and hide within my comfortable campsite, shutting out the adult world around me. But this old, straw mat of Sam's dependence—of needing me—I could no longer hide within it or drag it around Linus-like into the sanctuary of life.

And in spite of my lingering pain.

In spite of how much easier it would have been to bury my head underneath Sam's pillow.

In spite of my trepidation which this fresh freedom had flung at me, I stretched my hand upward with a resounding "Yes!" while His inviting directive pulled me up straight and standing.

Walking toward the door of Sam's room, I remembered his uncontainable grin after he had finally aced the road test. I remembered his victorious delight as he accelerated alone toward his high school.

And I knew.

I knew that Sam's joy was being offered to me, too. After all, it was a Sabbath, of sorts.

A "first day" for Sam.

And a "first day" for me.

A perfect day for picking up pallets.

And a perfect day for hiking on an unfamiliar trail.

Lord, teach us to pray . . .

Luke 11:1

Scriptural References
Luke 1:1–38
Exodus 26:31–33
Exodus 30:1–8, 34–37

Matthew 2
Mark 5:1–20
Revelation 5:8–10

Luke 2:21–31
Genesis 29–30
Jonah 1:1–3
1 Samuel 1
Matthew 6:9–13

The Annual Christmas Letter

BUMPING INTO GABRIEL

My pacing and praying and praying and pacing had been intensifying. Too much time had elapsed since Zach's sad and surreal phone call, telling me he was on his way to my house.

Telling me he had lost his job.

His job that he loved.

His job which he certainly needed, with the hefty car notes for his nice, new car (the just-as-hefty insurance payments to go with it) alongside his living expenses for the apartment he had been sharing with his friend for barely six weeks.

When I finally heard Zach's footsteps coming through the back door, my body went limp with relief. Wearing his goofy winter hat with the warm earflaps, he looked much younger than the nineteen years he would turn in two days. His long, tight hug which had greeted me made him seem even younger.

I was not expecting the quivering words which slowly, unsteadily stepped out from his fearful face, informing me he had been pulled over on his way, clocked at 108 miles per hour, twelve less than the speed he had actually reached during his foolish display of intense frustration. His shaking statement sucker-punched me, knocking out any remnant of response I might have rehearsed during my fretful pacing and praying.

My mind was calculating his car note, his exponentially increased insurance payment, in addition to his three hundred fifty dollar speeding ticket—against my two-digit checking account balance—as he explained to me that he had been late for work one time too many, which was, according to him, the sum of two. Hiding his face in his trembling hands, he could not restrain the loud sobs which followed.

Neither could I.

As we wept together on my couch, my arm wrapped around his shuddering shoulders, every nerve ending in my maternal soul feeling the acute pain my son was—and would be—experiencing. While Zach agonized remorsefully over his mistakes, a tsunami of passion was surging within me, an urge to drive directly to his workplace and throw my body prostrate before his boss, begging him to reconsider, to give my son a second chance.

But even with Christmas just three weeks away, in spite of the overwhelming yearning within me, appropriate boundaries—not to mention Zach's potential mortification—banned me from such recourse.

Moms simply *cannot* intercede like that.

I was reminded of the helpless crowds of worshipers waiting outside the temple, wondering and worrying about Zacharias, who had been shrouded by purple and violet and scarlet far too long. They, too, had been prohibited from interceding, completely reliant upon their intercessor who alone burned pure perfume in the terrifying square where Holiest Mystery met with one man.

Zacharias . . .

On that day, however, as Zacharias tended the fragrant altar, he encountered a dreadfully different enigma. Positioned to the right of the smoldering incense was a formidable, magnificent creature. Eerily billowing smoke had surrounded the staggering angel when he had materialized, horrifying the elderly, trembling priest, convinced his death was imminent.

The otherworldly voice of this celestial being, however, regally reverberating against the flickering fire which illuminated the golden glow of the ark, spoke not words of death, but of promised life.

Life of a fervently prayed-for-son, the hope for whom had been rubbed away by too many childless, passing years.

But when this foreboding, heavenly dignitary proclaimed to Zacharias that his soon-to-be-born son, John, would become a heart-preparing, Lord-announcing, teetotaler of a prophet, Zacharias responded by uttering seven fateful, faithless words:

"How can I know this for certain?"

An indignant silence, which no clock could measure, hung suspended in the sacred space, floating hauntingly with the cloudy smoke until the imposing, divine messenger—his brilliance still radiating from his residence within the Transcendent Holy of Holies—revealed his identity. And the muteness which had prefaced Gabriel's pronouncement transferred to the devout-but-doubting priest, his wife and life too old for such a breathtaking impossibility.

Stupefied, Zacharias stumbled out to the perplexed, intercessor-dependent horde huddled outside of the place which they could never enter, gesturing like a manic mime, dramatizing the incredible, numinous event witnessed by only his eyes. Eyes desperately pleading for comprehension—for compassion—from those who were relying upon his mediating pleas.

It appeared the revered intercessor needed intercession . . .

Looking into Zach's watery, red eyes, I saw the same pleading desperation.

And I had felt it within my own heart.

Why did my faith, like a cowardly grunt, so quickly retreat the moment the perceptible posed as an indomitable foe? I felt powerless to bench-press the heaviness of depression descending upon us both, like the thick, crimson and lilac veil which had hidden Zacharias in that nexus of humanity and Holiness.

Maybe I was too much like Zacharias, preferring prove-it-to-me, cast-iron sureness over the illogical, confident calmness which Mary had shown when Gabriel had visited her several months after his disappointing dialogue with Zacharias.

Expressing curiosity—not incredulity—Mary had believed the marvelous, mindboggling revelation of Gabriel, wondering out loud, not if she would bear the Son of the Most High, but how God would accomplish this through a virgin.

I wanted her simple, hope-holding faith as I sat close to Zach in this uncomfortable, I-want-to-know-for-certain moment.

What gave Mary that sweet, surrendering certitude which Zacharias had lacked?

It would seem that the sudden, unexpected appearance of a stunning, supernatural celebrity would have been corroboration enough for the angel's astounding messages, but it did not meet the burden of proof for Zacharias.

Gabriel had exuberantly greeted Mary as the favored one—a salutation which Zacharias, as a priest, would not have required—and assuredly declared that God was with her. And Mary had pondered Gabriel's address, allowing his words to soak her heart like Zach's tears had saturated mine.

"Favored one."

"The Lord is with you."

"Mary."

I had wanted a fix-it-fast solution for Zach. A way out had felt as impossible as a barren, elderly woman bearing the prophet of the Most High.

As impossible as an innocent, young virgin becoming pregnant with the Son of the Most High.

But in reconsidering Gabriel's words to Mary, I had pondered them, too.

"Favored one."

"The Lord is with you."

"Lisa."

It felt as if Gabriel had crashed into this confounding corner of our lives, daring me to believe those dumbfounding words which he had spoken to Mary. As if he had ambled into our living room and thundered,

"Fear not!"

I am, after all—like Zach, like all His children—His favorite. And He is, after all, With Us.

The drapery of despair which had separated us from hope began to unravel, and I grabbed Zach's unsteady hands and spoke Gabriel-like words, informing him that, though it may not be easy, nothing will be impossible with God.

Then I pulled Zach close to me, kissed his forehead, and prayed over him.

Because moms *can* intercede like that.

MALE MASSACRES

Glancing at the running faucet in Taylor's bathroom sink, my eyes turned hastily to survey his bedroom. A random upheaval marked this area, as if seismic shocks had seized the small space and littered the carpet with odd fragments and torn pieces of trash. Alerting Taylor to the soon-to-be-spilling-over water, I was unnerved by the annoyed-yet-vacant stare he directed at me before picking up a straw from the dirty floor. He immersed one end of the straw into the sink, and took a long sip from the above-water tip of the straw.

As I listened to his confused, confusing talk, I had noticed his mismatched, baggy fleece pants and checkered flannel shirt, inside-out and haphazardly buttoned. It was just his monthly manic episode, nothing more, he had informed me, and he had not had any meds for months. When I cautiously, kindly whispered that he needed some help, his eyes became as dark and disturbing as the macabre posters which still remained on his wall.

Nausea and anguish bled within me, as if the shards from my shattering heart were slitting my soul. Following Taylor into the living room, he began accusing his father—who appeared intoxicated as he sat red-faced on the couch—of the same daily Jekyll-and-Hyde mood swings which I had endured for too many years. Cringing, I implored him as quietly as I could, to get out.

But Taylor, at twenty-three, had been enmeshed in this poisonous pathos for over a decade, rendering me powerless to enforce my entreaty.

When their angry yelling began to escalate, I nodded to Sam who had accompanied me on this wretched visit, and we did what I had begged Taylor to do.

We got out.

Few words passed between Sam and me as we drove home. It seemed like the earthquake which had ripped through Taylor's chaotic bedroom had ruptured a fault line throughout my whole being. Compounding the fracture, the anniversary of Jacob's death had hammered a stake on this very same day— just a couple of days before Christmas—and I felt almost as bereft of Taylor as I was of my firstborn son.

I could not help but remember those mourning mothers of Bethlehem, though no nativity set would ever include such grief-stricken, empty-armed figurines among the anachronistic wise men standing stately in the stable with their extravagant gifts cradled in their hands.

Yet what brutal horror was appended—though rarely mentioned—to the actual narrative of the unnumbered, star-following magi. After inquiring in Jerusalem about the new Jewish king, they were interrogated by Herod, the current crowned aristocrat who became insanely anxious about this potential threat to his throne.

And when the divinely forewarned, astute astronomers bypassed Herod, who had requested from them the location of this worship-worthy Babe, the resentful ruler became hysterically—and tragically—livid.

I could hear the hair-raising screams of frantic women, as the madman's minions marched into Bethlehem, barging through doors as mothers nursed, scanning the soon-to-be-bloodied landscape where children were playing, and slaughtering any tiny boy-child they guessed to be two innocent years or younger.

Evil had perniciously punctuated the sweet Christmas story, while siblings hid in shocked terror, and protective fathers futilely resisted the heinous henchmen who had come to murder their wee Jewish heirs.

A tremor of blackness had erupted in Bethlehem, swallowing up life as it shook. It seemed the dark forces opposing this Christ-Child were stepping into formation, the very forces which would culminate their campaign at His crucifixion, the subterfuge for their own defeat.

But it was the spine-chilling wailing of those mothers— the anguished women who bore the brunt of evil's assault, their lives forever haunted by the massacre of their sons— which echoed from the ancient prophet's mouth to the lips of my own soul.

It was as if there were maniacally jealous Herods seeking to slay my peculiar, pitiable Taylor. Herods sending out strange soldiers, saluting Nazi-like as they brandished their weird weapons.

The sharp swords of Bipolar and Anxiety Disorders.

The strangle-hold of Methadone addiction.

The toxic, paternal enabling.

The blunt blows of destroying demons.

Was I to be among the grieving mothers of Bethlehem, watching wide-eyed as they gruesomely murdered my son?

And I wondered about another mother, a Gerasene mom, unmentioned, but perhaps watching nonetheless. Watching as her crazed, uncontainable son—controlled by many filthy spirits—gouged himself with sharp, mountain stones, howling hyena-like among the dead, his eerie screams possibly reaching even his mother's ears. With no psychiatrists or sedatives, no stronger man to prevail, surely she, too, would despairingly witness the butchery of her son.

And she surely would have.

Except a boat had arrived on the shores of her pig-plentiful country.

A boat carrying Jesus.

A lifeboat, one might say.

Seeing Jesus from a distance—as the magi had seen the star—
the rock-gashing demoniac appeared more wise man than
lunatic; he hurried to meet the Christ-Child-now-Man, and
fell down at His feet.

And in the time it took for two thousand, demon-driven swine
to stampede into the sea, the as-good-as-dead demoniac had
become as-good-as-new. So new, in fact, he had wanted to tag
along with Jesus instead of remaining among the reminders of
his flat-lined existence.

But Jesus had refused the grateful Gentile's request; instead, He
had directed the newly animated man to go home.

Go home to share his incredible, God's-kingdom-has-come,
mercy-drenched story.

Go home to where, perhaps, his mother had been helplessly,
hopelessly waiting.

Go home.

That was what Sam and I had done, too, though it felt as
if we had left Taylor behind to dwell among the tombs,
waiting for the black tremors of Bethlehem to swallow up his
bleeding being.

When Taylor called the next day, I enthusiastically told him
about a community program which offered the help he needed.

But he alleged he had just seen the psychiatrist. New medications had been prescribed. All was well.

Discouraged, I hung up, fully aware that all was not at all well. The cycle would be repeated.

And repeated.

I stared at my cellphone, its blank screen mocking my previous phone conversation with the inviting woman who supervised the support program for which Taylor was a likely candidate. A program designed to point its participants toward independence.

Toward life.

Toward a direction Taylor was presently unwilling to walk.

And I understood the helplessness and hopelessness of those Bethlehem moms, powerless to prevent the marauding killers from slaying their precious, little boys.

I understood the helplessness and hopelessness of the Gerasene mother of the delirious, self-destructive demoniac before Jesus had pulled ashore.

I thought again of those magi, the wise guys whose inquisitive queries had led to Herod's lethal tantrum. It had almost seemed that their worship of and gifts to the Christ-Child were more crucial and critical than the breath of baby boys. Than the suffering sorrow of their defenseless mothers.

But I also thought again of Jesus, stepping out of the boat into a God-less country of unclean animals and filthy spirits—a country where evil ran rampant like rabid wolves—and calming and curing the once-violent tomb-dweller before being chased away by the pork-dependent denizens.

I thought of Jesus, Lord of Life, emerging from the tomb Himself, shifting the tectonic plates of the cosmos, reclaiming His good creation, and massacring evil itself.

I was certain, then, that those mysterious, night-sky gazers from the East had offered their worship and gifts because the breath of boys, the torment of men, and the anguish of mothers mattered immeasurably to the rescuing Messiah they had finally found.

And because He is worship-worthy, I was not helplessly, hopelessly paralyzed as I experienced this devastating-but-dwindling darkness stomping into my sphere.

I was not alone and incapacitated, passively wringing my hands, waiting and worrying about stone-slashing sons.

No!

Jesus has already planted His feet upon the beachhead, and the aftershocks from His footfalls are downing Herods and drowning herds.

And because His kingdom has arrived, I will fall down with those rejoicing, Gentile astrophysicists.

I will fall down with the unshackled, once-shrieking demoniac.

And I will fall down with the twenty-four elders with golden bowls full of the prayers of the saints—full of my prayers—and sing a new song of worship.

"Worthy are You, for You have made Your saints to be a kingdom and priests to our God, and they will reign upon the earth."

Because moms *can* intercede like that.

EPIPHANY

As I was pouring my morning cup of coffee, I noticed a small mess on the dining room table. A handful of empty, foil wrappers from half-price Christmas candy was strewn like confetti around an orange juice bottle, holding no more than a gulp of the tangy-sweet liquid. Although we had just welcomed in the New Year, it looked as if Sam had held his own supplemental celebration, solo, sometime during the middle of the night.

After Sam had awakened from his sugar-coated dreams, I asked him if he had noticed an unruly pack of carbohydrates escaping under the cover of darkness from their shiny prisons and plastic constraints. In Mach speed, his shields of justification were airborne: His blood sugar had been normal, he explained, but he had programmed his pump to administer a few units of insulin for a late-night snack.

But a small dose of insulin was distressingly inadequate to cover Sam's dangerous nocturnal noshing, and I gravely expressed my concerns over his excessive consumption of carbohydrates.

Dropping his defensive front, Sam—at a velocity far exceeding

187

sound—shifted to a viciously offensive attack, f-bombs being thrown like hand grenades while he demolished my motherhood and cursed my pathetic life before decapitating my gasping spirit with his callous declaration that I would always be, and would die, alone.

Alone.

Though I was conditioned to the weight of that word, it threatened to bury me on that day with constant shovelfuls of its suffocating unwieldiness.

Of its too-close proximity to my daily reality.

It was a word which another woman had lived with for most of her adulthood. An odd, old woman named Anna . . .

> A prophetess she was, at a time when God had been as silent as my saddened state had become. Widowed as a young woman, childless and probably barren, she traced her lineage back to the tribe of Asher.
>
> Asher, second son of Zilpah.
>
> Zilpah, maid of Leah.
>
> Leah, the unloved wife of Jacob.
>
> Anna—hidden from the dictates of the outside world, from an economy which had deemed her worthless—had abandoned herself to an outer court cornered by four lampstands, standing like

sentinels guarding the temple from any access by women.

The constant chaos streaming in and out of the congested square—the bartering for altar-bound animals and the dutiful preoccupation with Levitical obligations—usually whirred right by this solitary figure, her thin frame as wiry as her wild and whitened hair, hiding her wizened face bent ground-ward, her lips incessantly mouthing words no one, but One, could hear.

Having spent over half of a century praying and fasting, looking expectantly for The Redemption, this weird woman had grown accustomed to the stench of slaughtered sacrifices and the dismissive, on-the-go crowds To most, perhaps, Anna's worshipful waiting appeared to be a woeful waste of her life . . .

A woeful waste of life. That certainly conveyed Sam's assessment of me, as he had so hurtfully expressed in his invective. And though I would have to address Sam's extreme and abusive disrespect, I had begun to ponder what else God was revealing through my son's ruthless rant—whether I would continue to lick my oozing wounds, spiraling deeper toward dark dead-ends or seek a deeper purpose than this darkness was purporting.

What aberrant bacteria had provoked such visceral vomiting from my logical, unemotional son? I considered the all-too-recent encounter we had both witnessed between his father and Taylor, how Sam had emphatically told me afterwards that he had wanted nothing to do with his Dad.

And I reflected on how incredibly difficult it had been for Sam—braving diabetes with lingering fears of low, midnight blood sugars, and facing adolescence, its facial hair and college considerations—without an engaged father to manly guide him along.

But mostly I had examined me.

Worn down by Sam's stalwartly stubborn resistance, I had long relinquished mandatory church attendance and had gradually given up on any spiritual readings and discussions I had attempted at home. Actually, I had just given up; Sam's surly responses to most of my requests, as well as my attempts at conversation, had me running Jonah-like from my own little Nineveh. I had even stopped asking Sam to occasionally share together the meals which I had prepared.

Indeed, alone was exactly how I had felt, especially when Sam was home.

Like solitary Anna, I had prayed, but certainly not with her relentless faithfulness. And not with her humble, incessant anticipation for The Redemption to appear . . .

> In a crazy, incredible convergence—a moment no man could have manufactured—the lives of the expectant collided with the two parents who had not expected to be greeted by such strange seers when they came to the temple to dedicate their firstborn son.

Who had not expected the shaking furrowed hands of venerable, Spirit-shadowing, prepared-for-death Simeon to take hold of their precious baby, Jesus, and to speak such marvelous, painful words.

Who had not expected, as Simeon stared sorrowfully into Mary's eyes, to be joined by aged Anna, bolstering Simeon's prophecy with joyous proclamations of gratitude for The Redemption finally embraced in Simeon's arms . . .

I, too, had not expected. Nor had I required much of anything lately from Sam. Acquiescing to the status quo—to a teenager who wanted me to leave him alone—I had lamely accepted that he and I were as good as it was going to get, half-heartedly asking God to intervene in Sam's life.

Somehow.

Some way.

And through someone else.

In the process, I was not expecting—or requiring—much from myself in our relationship. It had been easier, yet not-so-easy, that way.

Reluctantly, I headed upstairs to Sam's room. He had assured me he had been keeping it clean, and, shamefully, in my passive posture, I had blindly, foolishly, accepted his word. Taking a deep breath, I opened the door to his bedroom. The sight of Taylor's room on that not-so-long-ago night quickly claimed a very distant, second place compared to the condition of Sam's blue-ribbon disarray.

But strangely, standing in the middle of Sam's disgusting, suitable-for-only-mangy-dogs-in-subzero-temperatures room, I became acutely aware of the One Who never shies away from big messes, never shames us for making them.

And I had a revelation.

My defeated depression had not destined me to perpetual aloneness; Sam's razing tantrum and rebellious untidiness (though that is too prim a descriptor) had not doomed him to eternal hell—though he probably needed to be singed a bit. They were, rather, the urgent radiology reports placed on the backlight by the Specialist—never a comfortable or convenient consultation.

But always a critically necessary one.

Certainly Sam needed to seek forgiveness, yet, I contritely recognized, so did I. And as I confessed to the Forgiver, my tears of dismal desperation became drops of astonished gratitude.

Sam and I had been—in an unconventional, unexpected way—handed a second chance.

When my effusive feelings had tapered, I sat down with Sam, who listened quietly as I explained to him that his paternal legacy of abusive men was ending with my sons.

With him.

I reminded him of his namesake, Samuel, the son of Hannah, whose name, ironically was identical to Anna, meaning Gracious, and whose story was strikingly similar, too.

I reminded him that Samuel, like him, had been happily wanted. Had been prayed for passionately. And had been dedicated to God.

I reminded him that Samuel had become the great prophet who had anointed David as king when other candidates had appeared more appealing.

With just a silent nod, Sam agreed when I informed him that my longstanding threat would now be followed through: he would be cleaning out his old room, and moving into the downstairs bedroom.

And it seemed as if Anna had joined us at the table, silently nodding at me, too, and encouraging me to not lose heart.

Charging me to keep the faith with Sam.

Assuring me I would see his redemption.

And if, for over fifty years, this beautifully alone, humbly tenacious and powerfully peculiar woman could actively, hopefully, pray and wait, so could I. I could almost feel her elbowing me, as if to remind me that the guarding quartet of lampstands had been bulldozed.

As if to make me wonder what might have happened if she had not expectantly fasted and petitioned the Lord.

I looked directly into Sam's eyes, overcome by how tremendously I loved this son of mine.

Overcome by how tremendously God loved this often faithless daughter of His.

Revived by fresh—though not new—purpose I told Sam we would be talking each week about what it meant to follow Jesus. When I invited him to pray with me, he reflexively balked, his agitation apparent.

So I paused long and soft and hushed.

Slowly, deliberately, I began to pray.

"*Our* Father, You are in heaven. Hallowed is Your name."

I stopped again, allowing the words to release their breath, sensing Life rushing into the room.

"Your kingdom come. Your will be done."

My heartbeat was augmenting this invocation, imploring the True Father to bring His kingdom and His will to our Sam.

"On earth as it is in heaven."

And, in faith, I was confident the two realms had met and meshed in my modest, little living room through the sacred portal of prayer. I imagined Anna leaning over, smiling, and whispering into my ear,

"Moms *can* indeed intercede like that!"

P.S.

I was not certain if my tears had awakened me or if I had awakened and begun to cry. Or maybe it was the song playing in my drowsy head, its sonorous lyrics rousing me from dreams, reminding me of God's faithfulness. Sitting straight up in my bed, surrounded by darkness, I looked at my clock.

It was 2:30.

A.M.

Not the 5:30 I would have preferred.

Regardless, it was the tenth of the month, and the bill was due today.

Today.

The day when my bank account would boast a single-digit balance as soon as I paid the amount which was due.

Today.

The day that prayer was shaking my shoulders like a persistent alarm, mocking the futility of my feigned sleep.

It had been quite some time since I had visited this place. This place of looking up at night sky, straining to glimpse the silhouette of blackbird wings against the flickering apertures of waiting dawn.

I had not been financially careless or irresponsible; the sudden, unforeseen loss of income was out of my hands. But certainly not out of God's. And as I cried out to my Father, moonlight reminding me of His constant dependability, a parade of memories drum-rolled in front of me, each one trumpeting God's gracious—and often eleventh hour—provisions to us.

By the time I had dropped Sam off at school, I was more anxious about the incongruous peace which had replaced my wake-up worries than I was over my monetary conundrum.

Morning had almost relinquished the clock to the insistence of lunch when the delicate dinging of my cell phone pulled my sleeve. It was a text from Sam. Anticipating his usual "Bring insulin to the school now" message, my comprehension paused as I stared curiously at the unexpected request on the screen.

"Mom. My tax return was deposited. Transfer $400 to your account."

I read it again.

And again.

His gallant generosity boggled my mind. And my heart. But, reflexively, I almost declined his request. After all, I was the mom, and he was my son. My son who was still in high school. And I strongly desired to still be the one taking care of him.

Yet the odd timeliness of his noble offer, an offer not predicated upon his knowledge of my account balance, caused me to reconsider this regally beautiful blackbird which had flown in on an unlikely gust of grace. Grace not merely for me, but for Sam, whose heart was obviously being guided by the same, wild Wind.

Pecking out a reply of torrential gratitude to Sam, I pressed "Send," incredulous at the marvelous, beyond-my-imagination response of the God Who had stirred me from my sleep, nudging me to pray and prodding Sam to give.

Apparently it had been a bit breezy in Zach's neighborhood, too. Having had the day off, Zach whooshed through my door that afternoon and, after mentioning how much he was his enjoying his new job, handed me a crisp stack of twenty-dollar bills.

I was stunned.

In mere hours, I had gone from straining my eyes toward unlit heavens—hoping to somehow sight vague formations of flight— to gaping at raven feathers canvased on sun-splattered sky.

And I wondered.

These blackbirds and my boys? How had it so miraculously, so mysteriously happened, that these blackbirds *are* my boys?

Perhaps, when moms intercede, impossibilities inexplicably transmute into swooping crows, their beaks stuffed full by the hand of Our Father, delivering His faithfulness directly to our front door.

Today.

A man experiences redemption . . .
not by self-reliance, but by God-dependence.
Not by being true to himself, but by coming
to the end of himself. In the ruins of his own efforts
and ambitions, he meets God, Who comes
to meet him out of the holy wild.
"Come," He says. "Follow Me."

Mark Buchanan,
Your God is Too Safe

Scriptural References
Luke 5:1–11
Exodus 3
John 21:1–22

MOVEMENT FOURTEEN

Homily from an Old Boat

HOMILY FROM AN OLD BOAT

I could almost see the caseworker's yawning countenance through the receiver of my phone as I desperately explained my situation to her. She was not interested in my humiliating story, that my severe frugality had been no match for the significant loss of child support. That the only door of employment which had opened to my bruised knuckles was a temporary, no-benefits job at a large nursery and landscaping business. I had accepted this job with a lurking fear that my just-above-minimum wages would exceed the gaunt paucity which Sam's Medicaid mandated.

But that lurking fear had been more like a harbinger. The caseworker's apathy was flatly conveyed as she explained that loss of child support was not calculated as loss of income. That Sam's part-time earnings from Dairy Queen, coupled with my recent diminutive gross pay, had tipped their scales unfavorably. Incredulously, her tacit, finger-wagging message had seemed like a cold and crazy reprimand for my toiling hard hours on unforgiving concrete floors and sweating non-stop from heavy lifting and intense heat.

My throat constricted as I choked out a good-bye, reeling in the realization that only a tiny amount of insulin remained in Sam's last vial of life-saving liquid. A liquid with an exorbitant refill cost. As I hung my head in defeated frustration, I considered her parting advice: If I quit, it was possible that the annual pro rata of my meager two-months of income could reinstate Sam's medical insurance.

I was caught again in the classic conundrum of "damned if I do, damned if I don't."

In this stiff, red bureaucratic tape, I had felt helplessly trapped. Yet the perpetual pharmacological parameters governed by Sam's chronic disease were far more rigid, with its non-negotiable demands for quarterly check-ups, pump supplies, test strips, meters, lancets, and, of course, insulin. And in this do-or-die moment, Sam's immediate and urgent need for insulin muscularly trumped my need to work.

Work.

I had enjoyed the intense physicality. The simplicity of brown-bag lunches eaten outside under a shady tree. The ordinariness of my co-workers, their uncompensated glory hidden behind khaki shorts and dark green tee shirts stained with perspiration and potting soil. The much-anticipated showers which awaited a very grimy me at the end of every shift had reminded me of Peter . . .

> The morning tide was lapping against Peter's aching legs. His fatigued body smelled of murky lake water and a night's worth of futile exertion. After working the graveyard shift without pay, Peter was wearily

washing out his fishing nets, ineffective as they had been for him, probably wondering if there was more to life than the relentless uncertainty of biting fish and capricious profits.

More to life than the circadian stress of just getting by.

Of having enough.

Removing the last of the lake litter from the tangled web, Peter had only wanted to wrap up the cleaning details and head straight home for a quick breakfast and long nap. At least he could forget about the night's maddening disappointment and the day's lack of income. But as congested crowds began to congregate on the beach beside him—the pathetic seekers, the unemployed groupies, the curious miracle-chasers merging onto the sand behind The Master—Peter had wanted to escape even more.

Maybe Peter had wanted to escape life altogether.

He was tired.

Tired of too many fishless fishing expeditions.

Tired of the same ole, same ole.

And he was tired of these suffocating people, barking out their humiliating questions of "Catch any fish?" and "Where were the fish hiding, boys?"

He had tried to ignore them. Ignore the One they were trailing. The One Who was walking directly towards him, His eyes smiling as He asked Peter to hop back in the boat. To punt out a bit from shore.

The last thing Peter had wanted to do was get back into that God-forsaken, fish-shunning dinghy.

Peter had nodded, though. And as his aggravated spirit rolled its eyes, the pushing people pressed closer to the water's edge.

The last thing Peter had wanted to do was to listen to some preaching.

But as the current softly slapped against the rough wood of his old boat, water and Word swaying the floating pulpit, Peter's taut shoulders and heavy eyelids relaxed a little. And Peter was listening. After all, the throng of craning ears just a stone's throw away could not hear The Preacher more plainly than Peter.

It was a shallow-water sermon of puzzling parables and a priceless-pearl kingdom. A kingdom more like small seeds and free-spirited birds and grace-grown lilies. More like a fishnet catching all kinds of fish. Where one soul was worth more than an ocean of fish. Where a lost life is found and a found life is lost.

And now, as mounting sun was chasing away any experienced fishermen or expectant nibblers, no one could hear The Preacher more plainly than Peter as He instructed the exhausted, expert angler to paddle back out to deep water, to cast his nets once again. With hunger gnawing raw within his gut, and arms still burning from heaving nets and battling oars, the bass pro informed the Carpenter that they had been there.

Done that.

The last thing Peter had wanted to do was return to the mocking abyss.

But The Master had said so.

The Master Who had already renamed him as Rock.

The Master Who had already healed his feverish mother-in-law.

So, with palms like visors shading their eyes, the confused beachcombers and Peter's perplexed partners watched as a perturbed Peter turned his boat around, heading right back to where he had labored all night for nothing, and, per The Master's request, dropped his nets again. Except this time, instead of pulling up a limp, waterlogged net, Peter, his adrenaline suddenly revitalizing him, strained and tugged at a net ripping under the weight of incalculable, slithering grace . . .

Although Sam's Medicaid had been reinstated, my financial struggles had not magically been eliminated, and I was soon propelled into another just-above-minimum-wage job with zero medical benefits.

Again.

And Sam's Medicaid was terminated.

Again.

And I had applied to Medically Handicapped Children's Program for help with Sam's diabetic expenses.

Again.

And after returning from a Thanksgiving visit to my parents' home, Sam's last vial of insulin was almost empty.

Again.

When I called to check on the status of our application, the new caseworker had kindly informed me that Sam had been approved. But her sigh-of-relief words were quickly followed by her apologetic addendum: I would have to pay the first one-thousand dollars of his diabetic expenses before their program kicked in for Sam. Gratitude and panic were suspended within me. I was clueless as to how I would secure this sum—a small amount in the healthcare world, but an enormous fortune in mine.

But I remembered something.

During our good-byes at Thanksgiving, my dad—despite my protests—had tucked some folded money into my hand. Overwhelmed by the effusiveness of the moment, I had immediately slipped it inside my wallet, freeing my hands for hugging.

But now—with the near-empty bottle of insulin, and the caseworker's words reverberating through my shortened, anxious breaths—I recalled Daddy's gift, hiding and uncounted.

Pulling out the bundle of bills, I slowly unfolded them.

I was stunned.

Ten one-hundred dollar bills were smiling up at me!

I could not help but think of Peter, except this time he was reeling in a fine fish after only his first cast, a fish with its mouth bulging, a four-drachma coin concealed inside. The exact amount required at the exact time it was needed. Just as The Master had said.

But as business gradually dwindled at my job, so did my work load, shrinking until there was nothing to do except answer an occasional call or help an infrequent customer. Even after scavenging for menial tasks, almost the entire day was consumed by merely sitting at a desk, hopeful for a ringing phone or sporadic patron.

And my soul was shrinking right along with their expiring enterprise.

As I returned day after day after day to an empty to-do list, I had wondered about Peter, this professional—and yes, persistent and patient—fisherman who had logged innumerable hours trawling this lake.

Why had he not called it quits long before midnight had blurred into 6:00 A.M.? Surely he had recognized it was one of those nights, when even his favorite ace-in-the-hole, when-all-else-fails lure would not entice a single nip or glance from these evasive, finned creatures.

What driven desperation had eclipsed Peter's sound judgment, his rational respect for his cohorts? Again and again and again, a maniacal determination was hurling the nets into a stubborn, unyielding sea.

Was it doing the same to me?

Peter and I, we had wanted the same thing: an insurance policy. Or at least a nine-to-five which would guarantee tomorrow's security plus a little cushioning in the checking account. Guarantee that our pantries held more than mere daily bread. We wanted a life where faith was a nice, but unnecessary, concept, even if it meant compulsively casting ourselves into fishless waters until we were depleted and starving and too tired to trust.

But perhaps it was our depletion, our starvation, our exhaustion which had opened our ears to the homily from an old boat. Which had tugged us back out to the futile familiar, only to discover it was not about the fishing hole—or even the fish—

but about The Fish Whisperer.

Not about our dogged tenacity, but about our utter emptiness.

And Peter and I, we had done the same thing, recklessly casting ourselves at the knees of The Master, totally exposed by the net-ripping, boat-sinking, incomprehensible abundance thrashing all around, and summoned by the One Who sought out an obsessive, uncouth fisherman and a (somewhat) neurotic, discouraged woman.

By the One Who had dropped His net to our unfathomable depths and pulled us up with His unexpected response.

"Do not be afraid."

Afraid.

Peter and I, had we not both been fearfully flipping and flopping and flipping and flopping, like those wide-eyed fish tossed on the sand, their gills franticly expanding for one more moment of survival?

Was it always, *always* the fear?

The fear that there would never be enough, whether it was enough fish to feed the family or enough insulin for Sam.

Was not the insidious terror which had coerced a bleary-eyed, frenzied angler to keep casting and casting and casting, the same furtive fear which had dragged me to this deadening, dead-end desk duty, day after day after day?

I could not help but remember Moses, year after year after year passing as he pastured his father-in-law's sheep—until God showed up in a bewildering, burning bush. And with the kind of knowing which only comes through lonely decades of monotonous shepherding,

Or hundreds of crazed casts into dark waters . . .

Or the tenth anniversary of a divorce from an abusive marriage . . .

It had seemed that the Master had invited us away from the shallow shoreline of flocks and fish and mostly fear, and into the kind of unplumbed trust which had left the beach congregation baffled as they incredulously watched Peter & Company foolishly walk away from the dying, scaly windfall writhing in the sand.

Walk away from the first of a few fish feasts which Jesus would supply to some crowds who had liked His preaching.

Walk away from his family and the *only* livelihood he and his family—and his family's family—had ever known.

Walk away from everything.

The petulant Peter who had reluctantly shoved away from the shore—the one who would have opportunistically grabbed The Master as an entrepreneurial Fish Magnet—

was no longer the same man when he arrived back on the gritty beach.

Peter and I, we had been irresistibly drawn to the Beautiful God-Man, the One Who subdued not only fish, but fishermen and fearful moms.

What else could we do but follow The Master?

The Master Who had promised that others would be irresistibly drawn to the Him-in-us, too.

When I handed the typed notice to my employer, my hands were a little shaky, even though I had had no doubts that I had followed His leading. But I also was aware of something of which Peter had been completely unaware when critical crowds and smelly fish and torn nets and old boats were blurring behind him.

I knew that Peter would reenact the same drama. Confused and despondent and restless, he would fish and fish and fish all night.

Again.

After all, he had only seen the Resurrected Master two times over two weeks. And it had been easy for Peter to persuade a few downcast disciples to join him in the boat. But as they threw out their nets over and over and over, they caught absolutely nothing.

Again.

But in one of the most lachrymose moments of John's gospel—as night sky blended into the tangerine-pink of dawn—as the smoke of a charcoal fire mingled with the heady aroma of grilling fish and warming bread, The Master was watching from the beach. And with a wink in His voice he shouted out to them.

"Children!

"You do not have any fish, do you?"

"Cast your nets on the right side of the boat."

Immediately, 153 *large* fish were swallowed by their net, a net which strangely did *not* tear, although they were unable to haul it in.

And after feasting on the intimate breakfast which Jesus had served them, Peter was pulled away by The Master Who, as He questioned Peter's love for Him, addressed him over and over and over.

"Simon, son of John."

"Simon, son of John."

"Simon, son of John."

Those were the first words Jesus had ever spoken to Peter.

The words which had prefaced The Master's christening of Peter.

The words which had represented Peter's old name.

And with the kind of knowing which only an honest assessment of one's story can bring, I knew with certainty—though uncertain about what lay ahead—my own proclivity to climb back into old boats without Him, in spite of His bottomless faithfulness.

My own inclination to fearfully cast and cast and cast, pulling up nothing but distrust and faithlessness.

My own tendency to live from my old name.

As John closed his account of the breakfast on the beach, Peter and The Master were winding up this painful, though necessary, conversation. A conversation which had overshadowed Peter's ecstatic joy as he gamboled through the tide toward the Risen One. And though Peter's hunger had been satisfied, a huge mess of big fish are frantically flipping and flopping on the sand behind him.

Again.

And Jesus concluded by simply telling Peter to follow Him.

Again.

———◆◆———

Sam's insulin bottle is almost empty today, and the soft-spoken caseworker from Medically Handicapped Children's Program just called me. She told me I only had sixty-eight dollars left to pay, which is almost eight hundred dollars less than the cost of Sam's insulin.

I walk straight ahead, refusing to turn around where all my fears are wriggling in the sand behind me, their gills sharp and extended.

I breathe a prayer of thanks.

Borderland, that boat is. Refuge of the slow hearted.
The charter trip for those who want life
predictable, quiet, settled, safe—who want not to go out
to the deep, wild sea, but to hug the shore.
Who prefer a safe God who keeps his distance.

Mark Buchanan,
Your God is Too Safe

Scriptural References
Matthew 14
Matthew 8:23–27
Luke 15:11–31
Luke 24:36–44
Revelation 20:4; 21:1–5; 2
Revelation 21:1–5; 22:1–5

Note Worthy

NOTE WORTHY

The salesman had spotted me as soon as I walked through the massive glass doors, my trembling hands hiding my tear-drenched face. With cheetah-like speed, he escorted me into the glass-encased conference room, its see-through walls a sound barrier between my blatant begging, and the shiny cars and shinier salesmen on the other side. Like a crude cardboard sign held on a street corner, I pled with him to nullify the whole dreadful deal, to mercifully release my diabetic, man-acting teen from the iron-bars of debt which had been dead-bolted by my very own signature.

It had certainly not been my idea. Just the day before, Sam had announced that he would be getting a new car. Not brand new, but new enough. Not tomorrow. Not in the future. Today. Startled, I had volleyed with sensible advice:

"Wait."

I had explained to him there were many factors to research, to weigh, costly factors like interest rates and insurance costs. But Sam, impulsive, stubborn, and seventeen, had ignored my evaporating words.

And I—allowing him to navigate the perilous waters of adulthood, praying that financing would not be available for my money-making, risk-taking son—had surrendered the reins to Sam's wannabe manhood.

But when terror grabbed me by the shoulders at 3:30 in the still-dark morning, shaking me wide-awake from the brief intervals of numbness my fitful sleep had stingily allowed, the reality of that inversely answered prayer had dragged me into the kitchen. Turning on the switch to my coffeepot, I stood wobbly while water gurgled through caffeine, my regret as thick as the soggy, coffee grounds hidden within the filter.

I had slogged through my morning run as if I were desperately trying to outrun the panting panic breathing down the neck of my vulnerability. By the time I had arrived back home, the seizing fear, the shrieking what-ifs, and the spasms of shame propelled me to swipe the cursed keys from the kitchen counter and drive Sam's sporty, sleek debt straight to the dealership.

The dealership.

Where I had walked straight through those massive glass doors. Straight into the glass-encased conference room. The conference room where my pathetic petition was refused by a fancy suit and tie inhabited by a male young enough to be my son.

And after scraping my most mortifying moment off the polished, oval table, the transparent doors silently slid open, bidding my cringing humiliation farewell. Heading back home, I had anguished over the latitude I had handed to Sam.

Surely I was the one who had loosened the slipknot and sent Sam straight into those risky waters of adulthood. Into the looming danger which would inevitably sink us both.

I had wondered if that was how Peter had felt on that tempestuous night, the headwinds howling, the horrendous waves menacing the crew of disciples struggling against their own inevitable sinking, the impassable wall of water and wind threatening to pull the exhausted men right into the ghoulish sea . . .

> Their back-slapping merriment when they had shoved off from shore, their wacky grins as they recounted to one another how they had somehow filled each empty, reaching hand with each tearing of the loaf—it all seemed like a vaporous dream drowned by the crashing, cold water lapping about their ankles in their battered boat. The fish-n-bread feast they had handed out to thousands out in the middle of nowhere seemed like a surreal fantasy swooshed away by the fierce winds.

> And the twelve baskets of leftovers which had stuffed their bellies full felt as phantasmal as the apparition floating atop the wild whitecaps, coming right at them. If the surging storm did not snatch away their trembling-in-terror bodies, this ghastly, water-walking specter was certain to finish the job; either way, their greatest fears were no doubt becoming their fateful reality.

> Until, over the yowling gusts and crashing crests, the

ghostly figure shouted,

"Take courage, mates!"

"It is I!"

"Don't be afraid!"

It is I? Seriously?

Would it have been too much trouble to add an additional syllable and forthrightly state, "It is Jesus?"

Don't be afraid? Seriously?

Take away all those Sunday-school, felt board lessons with sweet, static cutouts of pretty blue waves and an easy-to-recognize Jesus, and this whole dramatic scene seemed more like an off-the-charts cruel joke.

But this real-life drama was neither poltergeist nor prank.

And Peter, frantic to know that the eerie form headed their way was undeniably Jesus, had cried out,

"Lord!"

"If it is You!"

Who would not have wanted a boatload of

reassurance in this perilous, crazy-making moment?

And with deadly gales and waves whipping around him, Peter yelled out what the silent eleven, in their paralyzing fright, could not.

Would not.

"Tell me to come to You on the water!"

Seriously?

Why in the world would Peter have requested *that* as the means for Jesus to prove His identity?

After all, this was not the first time Peter had been in unruly seas with Jesus. A Jesus Who had been snoozing soundly in the boat with them while they maniacally fought against the inevitable sinking. Incredulously, they had shaken Jesus awake, only to be scolded by a yawning Jesus for their faithless fear before He chastised the chaotic waters, subduing their drowning turbulence with simply His word.

Why had Peter not asked Jesus for one of those awesome, turbulence-subduing words, taking care of this identity-crisis and lethal squall all with a simple phrase?

Instead, Peter had asked his Rabbi for an invitation.

An invitation to join Him out on those hellish, heaving waves just as He had, hours earlier, invited

222

Peter to miraculously feed the thousands of starving seekers who had tracked Jesus to the desolate place.

And now, in a vastly different desolate place, the Rabbi was beckoning Peter once again into the impossible.

"Come!"

And to the bug-eyed dread of the eleven muted men (Were they speechless, or had they screamed at Peter, hysterically pleading with him to remain in the only ostensibly safe spot, the boat?), Peter alone had hefted himself over wet wood, landing on his feet, facing the water-walking One Who was summoning him!

How many incredible steps had Peter taken before the invisible wind shrieked louder than the Real One calmly bidding Peter to come?

How many skimming strides had Peter taken before he screamed,

"Lord!"

"Save me!"

And without a moment's hesitation, Jesus had done exactly that, catching Peter with His outstretched hand . . .

I needed that—that outstretched Hand—to rescue me from this

chaotic storm churning within me.

From this boat-sinking specter inevitably headed my way.

I bent down by my bookcase, and ran my finger across the spines, seeking a subduing word from one of my faithful friends. Unexpectedly, my hand halted at C.S. Lewis' celebrated *Screwtape Letters*.

It had seemed like an odd selection. But the clever correspondence between cunning Uncle Screwtape and his sophomoric demon, Wormwood, was like a soothing voice coaxing me out of my porous, parsimonious little boat. Lewis had so incisively named it, my bone-shaking trepidation, my shivering anxiety, now naked and precise in the eye of this hurricane: my fear of the future.

Or, as ol' Screwtape had succinctly named it, the "unreality" called tomorrow.

How had I so quickly—on the heels of the old boat's homily, of the blackbirds' whooshing wings—written and starred in a futuristic horror flick, complete with an apocalyptic ending?

Why, *Why,* do the words of the psalmists sound more like the eerie moaning of a fictional ghoul when my deflating life-raft starts filling with the phobic saltwater of dread?

Why, *Why,* in my gospel-less angst, is a miraculous appearance of Jesus not what I am expecting?

For Jesus and His twelve talmidim, the day had certainly not unfolded in the way they had expected. The preparer of The Way had died, and now The Way was preparing Himself to die. He was feeling the full weight of His ultimate vocation, and He had needed some serious silence and solitude following the gruesome death of His beloved baptizer, John.

And in the wake of the Baptist's cruel beheading, the twelve talmidim—a bit frightened themselves—also needed to grieve his loss. To rest with just Jesus without the needy assortment of tag-alongs robbing them of some reassuring quality time with their Master.

But the needy assortment of tag-alongs had done just that, snatching away their cozy, restorative men's retreat by beating them on foot to the hoped-for sanctuary they had rowed over to on the lake.

Or had it been Jesus' tireless compassion which had sabotaged their spa-day, His tender love unable to resist the countless sick among the arriving masses?

Surely after a full day of touching and being touched, of feeling the hurts of so many, Jesus—His humanity prone to fatigue—would shoo away the hungry hordes, away from the tired disciples, away to the vendors hawking day-old loaves and salty sardines before sunset.

But He did not.

The soon-to-be Broken Bread had broken bread instead, and the twelve weary, broken men had taken two tiny fish and five simple loaves and served the entire needy assortment of tag-alongs.

And instead of shooing away the crowds, Jesus had shooed His disciples away from the crowds. Away to the savage storm waiting for them on the sea. And after graciously and personally dismissing the crowds, Jesus had stayed there.

At the desolate place.

Praying.

Alone.

In the dark.

Until after the third watch of the night, when Jesus had sauntered out to them, His feet striking the water as if on the sandy shore.

And His talmidim were not expecting Him.

At all.

Consumed with the unrelenting assault of water and wind, they would never have anticipated—even in their most unrestrained imaginations, even after the most recent, outrageous miracle they themselves had participated in—Jesus meeting them in the middle of a choppy, churning sea, looking more like specter than Savior.

And even in their most bizarre nightmare, the old salts would have never foreseen Peter, a willing man-overboard, abandoning ship and stepping out on water wilder than any dream.

They would have never conceived their Rabbi, already performing a magician's dream-come-true, to have rescued the sinking, drowning Peter with mere sleight of hand.

Yet, with the squall still raging all around them, with the drenched and direful eleven gaping in disbelief with one eye, and battling the monstrous ambush of water and wind with the other, He had.

And—as if this strange spectacle could possibly have become more baffling—Jesus had not reprimanded the violent sea, but had admonished Peter for his wee faith and show-stopping doubt.

Seriously?

This was a coast-guard-worthy, life-or-death moment.

And Peter had passionately—albeit impetuously—baled from boat and boys at the bidding of his Rabbi. Peter was walking the talk—and on top of water at that—and no one else had dared to join him.

Who would not have been distracted by the knock-you-down gales grimacing down at Peter?

But Jesus offered no attaboy. No pat on the back for his short-lived, solo courage. Not even a word of sympathetic consolation for his human shortcomings.

Instead, Jesus had responded with a concise, almost cutting—considering the circumstances—characterization of the one who had ventured from security.

"You of little faith."

"Why did you doubt?"

Was there a pang of hurt in Jesus' voice, barely detectable above the raucous cacophony of crashing water and thrashing wind? Perhaps a quizzical nuance within His question, wondering what had happened to Peter's confidence in His goodness, His love?

Or was there an undertone of perplexity within His eight words, wondering why—after the banquet by the beach—Peter had failed to understand that life in Him, with Him, had opened up a new Way to live.

In the here and now.

Regardless of five fish or fifty thousand.

Regardless of smooth or stormy sailing.

To live, not as victims of wayward winds or wicked waves, but as those who walk freely upon the truest reality of light and love and hope.

It seemed that Jesus was addressing me, too.

Me, the flailing one with microscopic faith, my internal chaos swirling out-of-control into a make-believe unreality based on my own self-editing.

At least Peter had been facing a real-time, body-endangering crisis.

But both of us, in perceiving our crises as solid actuality, had identified Jesus as an illusory ghost.

Maybe Jesus was questioning me, too, asking me why I had doubted. And in His gentle query, I quietly, deferentially, flipped the inquiry back to Him.

"Lord, why did I doubt?"

My thoughts sailed backwards sixteen years. I was standing at the kitchen counter with Sam, a toddling one-year old, on my hip. I had just done something I was not allowed to do during my marriage. Check the mail. My sons' father, then my husband, was not at home. A temporary restraining order had been issued against him after a drunken rage, granting me a brief reprieve from his constant abuse.

The liberating pleasure of looking through mail, however, had immediately turned to sickening shock. There were credit card bills for thousands and thousands of dollars, mostly from cash withdrawals he had made. Without my knowledge.

And his credit card debt was layered upon the thousands and thousands he had borrowed from a business partner whom he had never intended to repay.

I saw myself a few days later, nervously facing the judge while the church men stood in the back of the courtroom, their crossed arms and glaring faces commanding me to assure the judge that I wanted my husband back home.

And I submitted to their scowls.

I saw Zach and Taylor, just little boys, and me, still nursing Sam. We were homeless, suffering under their father's careless selfishness and enormous debt, living wherever we could. And

I was still cowering under the indelible scowl of the church men, believing that God would have scowled at me, too, had I packed up and left this wounding man.

Five more years would have to pass before the wounding man left us.

But now, with Sam's snazzy black car glancing at me from the driveway, I saw Him, His eyes holding both pain and love, His hand outstretched to me.

And just like Peter, I grabbed it.

I could see Peter, clambering back into the pitching boat with Jesus, collapsing and shivering, while the dumbfounded disciples huddled around them. And, as the night sky was lightening under dawn's tender nudge, the anarchy of weather ceased . . .

I glanced outside in the driveway at Sam's new car, which appeared to be just as eager as I was for Sam to return home from school. And as I awaited his return, I had recalled another father.

Not the father of my sons.

But a father who had financed his younger son's reckless, ruthless choice. A choice which had grieved this tradition-breaking, heartbroken dad so much that his parable could not contain the agony which his wealth-wasting younger son had brought upon him.

I, too, knew how much of Sam's hard-earned money would be

squandered on interest and gut-punching insurance premiums. How debt can become like ravenous swine feeding in a famished land. But I also knew our Sam.

I gripped the hand of the wave-striding, condemnation-free God-Man. The God-Man Whose grace is quicker and stronger than the scary seas clawing at our sinking feet.

When Sam barged through the back door, he found me right away. He was, of course, still puzzled by my schizophrenic morning and by my lack of confidence in his financial responsibility, which, he reminded me, had already been consistently demonstrated.

I was compelled, of course, to confess that my hyperbolized panic and skimpy aplomb had not been about my uncertainty in his money management; it had been about my shaky, shoddy faith toward our All-Good God.

And Sam, in his usual matter-of-fact manner, began to lay out his ambitious repayment plan, addressing his overspending on unnecessary indulgences, his frequent frittering of time. When he had finished his impressive spiel (When had he grown so tall?), he looked squarely at me.

"It's going to be okay, Mom."

From the mouths of babes-no-longer babes, indeed!

He was right.

Things were going to be okay.

Easy? Probably not. But certainly they would be okay.

Sam went to his room to get ready for his shift at Dairy Queen. And I sat there considering how Matthew had concluded his story. The story beginning with the beheading of the Baptizer. The story closing with their boat cutting through motionless water at daybreak's pink promise and docking at Gennesaret.

Gennesaret.

Where the bone-weary men were met once again with desperately needy crowds. Where the compassionate Jesus once again healed the sick, even those begging to merely touch the fringe of His cloak. And I wondered if Peter, as he watched all the commotion at this lakeside village, had yearned, like me, for his hyperventilating unbelief to be completely gone for good.

To never return.

But, for Peter, it had returned. Those disciples were scared by the Ghost once more. The Ghost they had not recognized.

Again.

And the Resurrected Broken Bread, the Risen Wave Walker, had responded with the exact same words.

Again.

"Why did you doubt?"

"It is I!"

Meanwhile, back in my own Gennesaret, sitting at my dining room table, I recognized that the Rabbi of the Raging Seas and the Papa of the Parable, They are the same. And They are always coming out to us in unexpected ways, strutting on top of foaming, frantic waters, flinging Their arms open wide, reaching Their huge hands straight into our own, inviting us into the Impossible.

I walked back into the kitchen and noticed Sam's high-tech keys peering at me by the coffeepot. Picking them up, I brought them to Sam and placed them in his hand. Borrowing Sam's matter-of-fact manner, I smiled and looked him squarely in his eyes.

"You're right, Sam. Everything is going to be okay."

Because one day, the other side will truly, finally, and completely arrive here.

Here.

Where the beheaded will no longer be buried, but will reign with the Son of God.

Where the starved and sick of our Gennesarets will no longer need hand-outs or healing.

Where the sea will no longer pitch and moan because there will no longer be any sea.

In its place will be that crystal-clear current from the River of Life, rushing through the middle of the Holy City, cascading fresh from the very Throne of God, watering the Tree of Life. And the ethereal green of its healing leaves, the succulent sweetness from its twelve kinds of fruit—they will not be a rub-your-eyes phantasm.

They will be our truest reality.

I am betting, too, we won't need new cars. Maybe just a sleek catamaran.

Better yet, I think I will just take a walk with Peter. The see-through, glassy surface of the River of Life should make for a great hike.

Who is it Jesus said would be blessed? 'Those who mourn.'
We learn to look fully into our losses, not evade them.
By greeting life's pain with something other than denial
we may find something unexpected . . .
When we learn to move through suffering,
rather than avoid it, then we greet it differently . . .
We become willing to let it teach us.

Henry Nouwen,
Turn my Mourning into Dancing

Scriptural References
John 19:25-27, 38-42
John 12:1-8
John 3:1-21
John 12:24
Luke 13:19

Garden Spots

GARDEN SPOTS

Zach and I had shifted restlessly as another pack of unfamiliar names were summoned to the stage. Certificates of recognition and achievement were silently dispersed among the red-faced, beaming students. The crisp, white 8x11's were slipped wordlessly into their anonymous, open hands before queuing dress shoes and fancy heels to clunk and click back into the applauding auditorium.

By the time the handful of honorees in Sam's small group of aspiring business leaders shuffled across the polished wooden floor toward the podium, I was awaiting the same, impersonal congratulatory transaction for my last-born son.

But as the two presenting teachers began to speak about a particular student—a student whom they would have never, four years prior, voted as the most likely candidate to place first at the state conference, a student they would have never imagined placing in the finals at the international conference in California—my restlessness quickly shifted into a valiant, but futile, effort to defend my unabashed pride against the splatter of tears pooling in my smiling eyes.

I could not fight them back that evening, and I could not ward them off four days later as I watched our Sam file in among hundreds of peacock-postured seniors. Wearing Zach's hand-me-down red gown, he blended unnoticed among the blur of tassel-topped, crimson-capped heads scanning the packed gym for parents or loved ones who would later receive the ribboned, red rose clasped in the hands which would soon be clutching diplomas.

And it was that perfect scarlet blossom pressed hurriedly into my empty palms—a poignant preface to being gathered into Sam's arms for an uncommon embrace—which had unbraided my coifed composure. Had it not been barely yesterday when I had scooted between the row of folding chairs to receive the rouged bud and hasty hug from Zach?

I was as helpless in arresting the assertive tears now wetting my wrinkled countenance as I had been in halting the aggressive stride of time.

When had my youngest boy—the happy toddler Zach had so insistently potty-trained, the floundering school boy who had built massive forts from fallen limbs and scavenged sticks, the budding entrepreneur who had peddled ice-cold soda on neighborhood corners and lakefront parking lots—become this confident, college-bound man with a heart soft enough to give Richie gifts cards and rides to the store?

Scanning across the crowded gym of moms and dads and grandparents and guardians, as Kelly, my dear sister of a friend gently held her hands on my shoulder, I knew my own puzzled plaint was echoing through the souls of these spectators.

Yet how would I—me, the mother who has had the sacred and painstaking privilege of launching Samuel Wyatt onto his own, unique path—properly bury this no-longer-necessary role to which I had devoted seventeen and a half years?

How could I grieve this little death without it burying me?

I was reminded of the two men, both secret disciples of Jesus who had undertaken the most earthshaking interment ever: Joseph, the rich, righteous Arimathean religious leader who had refused to assent to the crucifixion; and Nicodemus, the night-visiting, Jewish ruler who had been perplexed by a serpentine Savior speaking of second births . . .

> Though the fearful Eleven—the ones who had openly shadowed the now-slain Messiah—had fled, the once shadow-seeking duo had openly, agonizingly, removed the bloody, barely-recognizable remains of the beautiful God-Man from the grotesque, thorny crown stabbing through His sacred, wounded head.
>
> From the smeared, splintered wood stuck to lacerated skin.
>
> From each repulsive stake gashed through His hands and feet.
>
> No longer concerned about ostracizing or ominous consequences, Joseph had courageously requested the pummeled and pierced body of The One he had furtively followed. And no-longer-nocturnal Nicodemus, with obvious forethought, had provided

enough fragrant, bitter myrrh and medicinal, healing aloes to befittingly entomb a king.

Using almost one hundred pounds of the aromatic mixture, the two prominent men had arduously wrapped their beloved Jesus, strip by strip by strip. Sometimes silent, sometimes sobbing, sometime softly speaking of sweet moments with Jesus, they reverently prepared the dead Messiah for His tomb, the new, never-used one in the garden. The one Joseph had so graciously given.

Had they even known of Lazarus' sister, Mary, who had mysteriously, shockingly, been the first one to prepare Jesus' body for burial? With her strangely stowed pint of pure nard poured out like prophecy all over His feet, her hair had anointed her Lord for entombment.

Had an evening breeze brushed against their exhaustion, their confusion, their gut-churning grief as they languidly carried the limp, lifeless Son of Man into the cool, rock-hewn dark?

Had Nicodemus been reminded of that tameless Spirit-Wind Who animates all kingdom dwellers, as they stared incredulously at the thickly shrouded Figure?

Had he wondered, while they laid Him at last on damp stone, how *this* cruel killing could possibly preface being born again? How *this* could possibly demonstrate God so loving the world, the world which was responsible for *this?*

In the wake of this hurricane of evil which had descended upon their Sabbath-preparing day, had they glanced around for that life-giving gust before shoving the heavy boulder over the only remaining shaft of light?

Sam met up with us outside, his leather-cased emancipation in tote. We all huddled beside the shady tree, Kelly snapping a few keepsakes with her camera as strong winds threatened to steal her attempts to capture what really cannot be adequately archived.

Sam left. There were graduation parties to attend.

I headed home.

Alone.

How would I take this hard and happy, this messy and magnificent, season of my life down from the solid, rough beams of beautifully peculiar grace?

I thought of Sam as a little boy, crawling into my bed in the middle of those infrequent nights when he was afraid.

I thought of Sam in junior high, preferring the companionship of the computer to friends—and all my worried efforts to prevent what I now know is his gift and passion.

I thought of Sam's first day of work at Dairy Queen, his polyester uniform morphing him mysteriously into manhood.

I thought of Sam, trying to hold back an irrepressible grin as he was being touted by the two teachers on the evening of the awards ceremony.

And as I reminisced, I could not help but backtrack a bit from Jesus' burial to His final words to the disciple whom Jesus loved.

To the mother who, as her heart shattered beside the cursed cross, wondered if *this* was what Gabriel could have possibly meant when the angelic messenger had promised her that her Son's kingdom would never end. If *this* was what Simeon had meant that a sword would pierce her own soul, for certainly it had?

Surely Mary must have reminisced as well, remembering how she had listened to the out-of-breath shepherds while she held the swaddled God-Infant, soon to be wrapped again by Joseph and Nicodemus. Remembering how He had run His hands, now hideously punctured, over the smooth surface of His first piece of woodwork.

Yet in her little death, inexpressibly more grievous than my own, His impenetrable agony was overshadowed by His infinite compassion for His mother, by His resolute responsibility as eldest Son. And by His incalculable expansion of family, the same family He had promised to Abraham when He led him out of Harran.

Despite this entombment of my own, this precious part of

motherhood which had so quickly ended, I knew His love had eclipsed my ache. And I knew He had, like He had with His own mother, already made provisions for my future, a future where I will no longer be a single Mom, but simply a single in an empty nest.

And like Nicodemus, Jesus is alongside me, having made the proper preparations, as if He deemed this ordinary, little death of mine worthy of a princess' burial, dipping all that He is asking me to release—strip by strip by strip—into the bittersweet fragrance of my past as the healing, medicinal aloes of my tears soak each swaddling ribbon He is passing over to me.

It is gusty again as I write this outside. And it is Memorial Day. A plump blackbird has perched upon my fence, facing me with his shiny ebony puffing up in the wild wind, the music to which my pansies and petunias are dancing erratically. And their blissful bending, like colorful, charismatic preachers, speaks again of Jesus' tomb, the never-been-used one which the wealthy Arimethean had given.

The one which was in a garden.

The garden in which the Lord of Life, His heart no longer beating, had become the lifeless Mustard Seed, the Grain of Wheat, concealed by countless, anointed bands and death's thick blackness.

Sam and I used to hunt for caches, hidden and buried to those without a GPS and a curious sense of adventure. How many years had it been since we had headed outside with coordinates and our cell phones, ready for geocaching victories?

I glance at my promise-preaching pansies. My laptop almost slams shut under the force of the invigorating gusts.

But still the tears come.

A pungency blends with the wind. The Resurrected One presses another drenched strip into my hands.

Yes, I am convinced that my empty nest, like an empty tomb, will sprout a tree so large and lush that blackbirds will come and nest in its branches.

But today, it is a day of preparation. Joseph and Nicodemus—and Mary the sister of Lazarus and Martha—they are my companions.

After all, royal burials require a little more time.

'While I am in the world, I am the Light of the world.'
When He had said this, He spat on the ground,
and made clay of the spittle, and applied the clay to his eyes.

John 9:5–6 NASB

Scriptural References
Matthew 15:21-28
Isaiah 61

MOVEMENT SEVENTEEN

Spit and Ashes

SPIT AND ASHES

It was an ordinary Sunday.

It was a Sunday like no other.

And I had believed my son. After all, I had been standing against the shadowy darkness, the black evil which, he had said, wanted to consume him.

The black evil which, he had said, shot out of that hospital room like a retreating, yellow-eyed hyena.

I had believed him because his eyes, once narrowed and crazed, had softened. His body, once tense and jerky, had relaxed.

I had not known what to do. Taylor had been pacing and growling like a savage, slapping himself in the face. All my coaxing, calming words had floated away unheard. I had tried to just hold him, hoping these fiendish outbursts would succumb to my embrace. Instead, my soothing hug was returned with frightening, python-like force.

It had seemed that demons were darkening Taylor's eyes, eerily rolling backwards in sync with his inexplicable snarling. And I found myself praying again with that Canaanite, crumb-craving, doggedly determined mom, though my desperate pleas, unlike hers, were silently screamed,

"Lord, Son of David, have mercy on me. My child is demon-possessed and suffering greatly."

Her darling daughter, my precious, eldest son. Both cruelly disturbed.

She and I. Both frantically breathing the same petition.

"Lord, help me."

Help was exactly what was needed when Taylor's bizarre antics had begun to blur with slurred speech threatening his own life and refusing to comply with our urgent appeals to get in the car and head to the hospital.

Help had come, though, when my frustrating, futile attempts at forcing my flesh-and-blood adult-child into the car were fulfilled by the police I had been constrained to call.

Standing beside his bed in the bare emergency room unit, I had watched Taylor as he finally slept, the domineering turpitude having surreptitiously slipped out the door. Occasionally the nurse would step in, check vitals, and assure Taylor that they were trying to find a recovery facility with an empty bed which could properly assess and treat him. And as the nurse spoke softly to Taylor, I caught myself quietly borrowing the age-old prayers, exhaling their timeless petitions,

"Lord, Son of David, have mercy on Taylor."

"Lord, help him."

And help had come. A recovery center was found. Taylor had smiled there. His childlike enthusiasm had poked its head out from his beautiful grin as he talked about starting a community day program he had learned about at the center.

But after a few days, after diagnoses and drugs were dispersed, he was released. And he never became involved in the day program.

Taylor had called me one morning, as he sometimes does when he returns from his daily trip to the methadone clinic. His dad had just bought him a new phone and a speaker. His psychiatrist had just upped his anti-anxiety dosage. Would I, he had asked, pay for his haircut?

After the call had ended, I pulled out my old, falling-apart Bible. I have another one, new and intact. But I wanted the comfort these worn and wrinkled pages offer me, the way the pages easily part at a particular prophetic passage, the one I had prayed so many times for Taylor.

It was not hard for me to imagine the shriveled ashes and bleak despair which Isaiah had described. It was, however, difficult to imagine this sooty residue—the stuff that seemed to constantly color Taylor's life—morphing mysteriously into hip-hop, or magnificently mutating into a glory-bestowing laurel.

Into clothes threaded with light.

Into a tall and sturdy oak tree, planted by the Lord.

But I had caught a glimpse of it one evening. The evening I had visited Taylor at the Recovery Center, watching him grin as he excitedly handed out to his new friend the rich, fudgy brownies I had baked for him. And there it was! The charred chalky powder of his loneliness swirling up from the once-stale air, rising into glittering flecks of belongingness.

And I had wondered if my sketches of that stately arbor, of a jeweled tiara, painted from my pastel palette of expectations, were anything like the peculiar, prismatic patchwork God was twisting into a turban around Taylor's thick hair.

Were they anything like the knotty, weathered and whimsical tree with leaves of vibrant, other-worldly hues which God was planting?

Today as I write this, it is an ordinary Sunday. But it is also a Sunday like no other. Because today is the day of the Lord's favor, the day the Lord is rebuilding ancient ruins and restoring places long devastated. Certainly Taylor is not exempt from this gorgeous hope.

Nor am I.

Taylor has already been back to the Recovery Center.

Again.

And this time his plan is to begin a different day program, the same one I had all but begged him to become involved in well over a year ago, a passage of time which had thrown my fitful faith—sometimes somewhat hopeful, sometimes nearly hopeless—into the fiery kiln.

Maybe my graven images of beauty had been thrown into that white-hot oven, too. Maybe my stick-figure expectations of a Taylor getting a job and getting off methadone were preventing me from seeing the miracle of life within and with him today.

And perhaps the smoky fragrance from the smoldering, slate remains of my crude charcoal drawings, drafted on rough, gritty papers, are wafting upward in brokenhearted longing to the very nostrils of God—the One Who exhales the ashy air, breathing out new songs for two-stepping.

Breathing out sparkling particles of light.

Or maybe He just scoops up a handful of the dark, disintegrated dust and spits into it, and He places it on the eyes of our hearts. Only then, perhaps, are we able to discover that the crown of beauty and garments of praise are hidden within our broken hearts, our afflictions, and our ashes.

I do not know exactly what transpired on that ordinary, not-so-ordinary Sunday. Methadone? Mental illness? Minions of death and destruction? All are likely perpetrators. But on *this* Sunday, today, as I type to try to translate the not-so-ordinary, ordinary Sunday, I realize it no longer matters.

For what matters is not the substance of our sooty vestiges or the composition of the tinder forming our primitive altars. What matters—perhaps the only thing which matters—is the very

Stuff and Essence of God, the One Who infuses Himself into the cremated corpses of our disorders and drug-dependence, of our godless goals and independent idolatry, and miraculously, mysteriously, forms His Life—His freestyle dance—in us.

I think again of that Canaanite mother. How long had she been waiting before Jesus showed up and transformed her darling daughter? Days? Months? Years?

As I place my hand over this chapter which Isaiah had penned, I wonder if that Canaanite mother had clutched these verses, too, as she desperately pled for her daughter. Like her, I am waiting and watching for the only One Who can release from darkness the prisoner.

For the only One Who can proclaim freedom to the captives.

To Taylor.

God became man to turn creatures into sons,
not simply to produce better men of the old kind
but to produce a new kind of man.
It is not like teaching a horse to jump better and better
but like turning a horse into a winged creature.

C.S. Lewis,
Mere Christianity

Scriptural References
Matthew 18:18
Exodus 3:5
Matthew 17:4
John 3:8
Luke 9:28-33

MOVEMENT EIGHTEEN

Another Black Bird

ANOTHER BLACK BIRD

I had unfolded my faded red camping chair. The sun was chasing shadows by the water's edge, the soft pushing of the lake on the grassy, raised bank coaxing me to sit. To stay. Toting my book bag, I had hiked down to the secluded inlet—the still waters where God had often led me—hopeful to hear from the Creator of this morning's glory. Autumn was jostling the lingering warmth of summer, and it seemed I was saying good-bye to both season and son under a turquoise sky waving its own farewell.

Taylor, at twenty, was leaving. Going away for a year. A year to break free from addiction.

Packing up my melancholy, I had lugged her to my freshwater sanctuary along with journal and pen and Bible, expecting some incisive introspection to abandon my sadness in the stalks of fading flowers along the path. Settling into the comfortable canvas, I opened up blue, worn leather to Jesus' words which Matthew had recorded.

"Whatever you bind on earth shall have been bound in heaven; whatever you loose on earth shall have been loosed in heaven."

I strained to excavate relevance to my today, checking the footnotes for the passage. "Loose" was substituted with "permit," and "bound" with "forbid." I preferred "loose." It sounded more liberating, reminding me of a child laughing, of letting go of a kite.

But as whimsical and wonderful as I had imagined this "loose," my spirit still felt bound. Depressed. Dull and unresponsive to the noisy, incessant splashing and flapping behind me. After long minutes of wringing the passage—intent on discovering some ethereal epiphany—I had ignored the divine commotion spattering right beside me in my otherwise serene setting. Finally, frustrated more from lack of revelation than lots of racket, I turned slightly to discover the disturber-of-the-peace.

Perched on a knobby stump protruding out of the water was a large, black bird. He appeared quite proud of his position on the petrified wood.

Pleased that I had finally paid attention to him.

Perturbed when he plopped back into the water.

And persistent when he performed several challenging stump jumps before landing again on the nubbin.

Occasionally the comical coot—after establishing a confident stance on the knotty platform—would spread his massive wings, fluttering them up and down, momentum building, only to flop back into the water.

Again.

I was captivated by the gymnastics of this weird waterfowl. By his unsuccessful efforts to fly. Uncertain how long I sat, amused and mesmerized by my unexpected companion, I was certain the antics of this winged creature—bound from flight—were preaching the message I had sought. Reluctant to depart from this sacred spot, to leave my assiduous, feathered friend, I slowly folded up my chair.

Stepping onto the overgrown trail leading away from the lake, I watched his theater one more time, smiling as the coruscating, waving water—uninhibited in its relaxed motion—presented an ironic backdrop for the thwarted coot. And as I unhurriedly headed back to the trailhead, I was reminded me of another holy encounter by quiet waters.

Summer had been yawning, warm and nearly worn-out. Nearly worn-out like Sam, not-quite-a-boy, not-yet-a-teen. Zach had been spreading wings of his own, his stretching wingspan pushing away Sam. Sam, his loyal, loving best friend and brother, now a nuisance and a scapegoat for Zach's adolescent anger. Anger as hot as the day Sam and I had ventured off to the Platte River.

Shallow and tepid as tub water, the cajoling current winked at Sam as he waded out into the brown water, animated by sunlight speckles and meandering movement. At Sam's urging, I cautiously followed, adjusting to the shifting, muddy bottom. To Sam's shifting, calming countenance. He sighted a sandy island in the middle of the river and pointed, setting our course as his spirit exhaled.

No nervous looks over his shoulder to gage his brother's reaction to his revelry. No anxious checking of his blood sugar as he immersed himself in this simple beauty. No one but me, lucky me, to witness his joy, his abandon.

Lying down in this tender tributary of contentment, Sam closed his eyes and declared our adventure was way better than any overcrowded amusement park, his arms weightless as he released into the persuasive undertow all his worries, their heaviness mysteriously floating away.

I could not resist his unnecessary plea to stay longer; I, too, was captured by the magic, my spirit no longer grounded by gravity. As we explored our aquatic refuge, my soul longed to remain here. Longed for Sam to endlessly stay in this place. A place removed from tensions of broken brotherly bonds and diabetic dilemmas.

A place where anxiety appeared forbidden. Where surrender seemed permitted . . .

———◆◆◆———

Too quickly, Taylor had left. Left an emptied room, a simile of my spirit. A Taylor-shaped crater from the meteoric crash of his summer residency with me. Mourning had hovered at my door, and I had bid her to come in. Bid her to sit beside and soothe me with a companionship which promised comfort's arrival.

Green had disappeared when I returned again to the lake trail, now hiding under leaves blown from immodest trees. The familiar path had beckoned me for a brisk walk, and I had succumbed, exhilarated by cooler air and faster pace. A pace that had propelled me past the holy ground, pushing me along, until the Unseen Voice halted me and urged me to go back.

So I backpedaled to the sacred path, tromping on dried-up remnants of summer's splendor before inexplicably stopping my descent to the lapping water upon the shore. Seconds after I had paused, I was startled by an explosive sound—as if fireworks had detonated upon the water—emanating from the inlet where the once-glassy surface had stirred from the sudden, strong south wind. Enormous, dark wings emerged, piercingly pounding the water before takeoff. Unbound, the black coot was soaring, tailwind lifting him skyward as he magnificently took flight.

Stunned, I held my breath, enthralled by his airborne grandeur. Grandeur which gradually crashed into the waiting lake, skillfully nose-diving as if the maneuver was well-rehearsed.

Dumbfounded, I could not move.

Could not remove my running shoes.

Could not criticize Peter, eager to pitch tents and camp out for a while up on the transfiguring mountain.

Dreamlike, I could not grasp, yet could not deny, the drama which His untamed Spirit—Who blows wherever He wishes—had ushered me into.

Me.

This weak-flying, stump-jumping rail—stultified by his species, whooshed up by wind—had revealed to me what my own wrenching exertion could not. I trembled timelessly in this transcendence before I hesitantly headed home.

Home, where Taylor did not return. Taylor—wings unhealed and pinioned—had remained only one week in the recovery program before taking forbidden flight and moving in with his father.

And all my expectations, my disappointments, my fears, came flopping down cumbersomely upon me, threatening to anchor me to a waterlogged stump.

But instead of futilely flapping, instead of repeatedly jumping with grimaced efforts, instead, I had imagined . . .

> I am floating, relaxed and Sam-like, in a relentless flow of grace. Waters deeper than my trust splash quietly on the shores of a distant islet. Surrendered to this moving stream, the current carries me to its sandy edge, where the tide playfully washes over my feet as I listen and wait for the rushing resonance of wind.
>
> When a tickling breeze crescendos into a glorious gust, I stretch out my arms, and, like deafening applause, I become airborne, flying in abandoned anticipation of another unleashing, blustery gale.
>
> And glancing back at distant turquoise, I can see

three black V's on the horizon.

My sons.

Soaring.

Author's Note

STILL MOVEMENT

In a couple of weeks, Zach will be moving out.

Again.

A couple weeks after Zach's departure, Sam will be moving into the dorm at the local university.

As I reflect back on the swift stream of time, the psychological rape from being stalked and the horror of the swatting—compressed into a sentence of domestic violence probation—seem so distant now. And the bridge of forgiveness is allowing Zach and Sam (and even myself) to forge a new kind of relationship with their father. What graces!

Yet even within this tiny, remaining window of sons living at home, their breathtaking independence has left me reeling a bit. Has left me occasionally longing for them to stay a while. To share a meal or linger in light-hearted conversation instead of dashing off as young men should.

It reminds me of the Samaritan folks in the city of Sychar, the ones introduced to Jesus by the thirsty woman at Jacob's well.

The ones who came to believe in Him through their own encounter with Jesus.

The ones so captivated by Him that they had implored Him to stay a while with them.

Them.

The ones who hated Jews and were hated by Jews. They had never met anyone—especially a Jewish Rabbi Who had deigned to hang out with them—like Jesus.

Jesus. Disarming, unhurried Jesus.

Lately, I find myself joining in their blatant begging, their unabashed entreaty for Jesus to stay a while. Joining in their delight over His surprised and happy smile as He agreed to their pleasing request.

I wonder if He had intended to stay two whole days with His new Sycharian friends, or if they were all—Jesus and the Samaritans—enjoying each other so much that the deadlines of time were erased.

Another scene comes to my mind from John's gospel: the story about Andrew and his fellow follower of John the Baptist, who, upon seeing Jesus, had proclaimed Him as the Lamb of God. Curious, Andrew and his companion had tagged Jesus, asking Him where He was staying.

I imagine Jesus, turning toward the two men—flashing the same gracious grin which had mesmerized the Samaritans, the smile that spilled out of His eyes—and eagerly inviting them to come and see. I doubt they had expected Jesus to spend the entire remainder of the day with them.

Jesus. Disarming, unhurried Jesus.

And I remember those forlorn travelers on the road to Emmaus, Cleopas and his companion, the foolish ones, like me, who were slow to believe. The Risen Jesus had merged into their journey, and explained to them everything in Scriptures concerning Himself! Imagine that!

But when they had reached Emmaus, Jesus continued to walk, as if His travels plans had not included a stop at this small village.

As if there is an unassuming modesty within this beautiful God-Man longing to be invited by us.

And they had. Luke's gospel tells us they urged him strongly,

"Stay with us, for it is nearly evening; the day is nearly over."

And He did.

Jesus. Disarming, unhurried Jesus.

Maybe the petitions of the spellbound Samaritan villagers, the Baptizer's boys, and the Emmaus duo were more rapt response than independent initiatives. More an echo of the invitation they imperceptibly sensed in the complete acceptance of His

Presence. The Presence Who, without words, bids us—longs for us—to stay a while with Him.

Dusk's tender breezes are shooing away the humid heat of this late-summer day, cooling me.

Comforting me.

Assuring me His Spirit-Wind is healing and hovering over this moment, moving—always moving—over the surface of the deep waters of my soul.

I sit—disarmed and unhurried, stilled by His movement—certain He is forming a blackbird out of me.

Oh, I almost forgot to tell you. Remember Sam's shiny, sleek debt. He had it paid off in four months! But that's another movement . . .

QUOTES

Buchanan, Mark. *Your God is Too Safe.* Sisters, Oregon. Multnomah Publishers, 2001.

Eldredge, John. *The Sacred Romance.* Nashville, Tennessee: Thomas Nelson, 1997.

Holy Bible: New American Standard Bible. 1995. LaHabra, CA: The Lockman Foundation.

Holy Bible: The Message (the Bible in contemparary language). 2005. Colorado Springs, CO: NavPress.

Homan, Daniel and Pratt, Lonni Collins. *Radical Hospitality: Benedict's Way of Love.* Brewster, Massachusetts: Paraclete Press, 2002.

Lewis, C.S. *Mere Christianity.* New York, New York: Harper-Collins, 1952.

Lewis, C.S. *The Screwtape Letters.* New York, New York: Harper-Collins, 1942.

Manning, Brennan. *The Signature of Jesus.* Sisters, Oregon: Multnomah Publishers, Inc. 1996.

Nouwen, Henri J.M. *The Return of the Prodigal Son.* New York, New York: Doubleday, 1992.

Nouwen, Henry. *Turn my Mourning Into Dancing.* Nashville, Tennessee: Word Publishing, 2001.

Wright, N.T. *Evil and the Justice of God.* Downers Grove, Illinois: InterVarsity Press, 2006.

Yancey, Philip. *What's So Amazing about Grace?* Grand Rapids, Michigan: Zondervan, 1997.

ACKNOWLEDGMENTS

The pointy fingernails of independent self-sufficiency are stubborn splinters embedded deep within me. Fortunately, the tweezers of life with God have yanked out most of them. Yet there remains a remnant within me that still squirms when pure grace is heaped upon me—no earning it. No baking a plate of cookies as if to tip the scales a bit so that my indebtedness is not so glaring.

So I am squirming before all of you lavish grace-givers who freely deposited your love, your time, your faith, your prayers, and your resources into my life and this manuscript as I place my empty hands and full heart before you and our Father. Though my most elegant expressions of gushing gratitude are primitive patois, I offer them anyway.

The companionship of books during the years *Blackbirds & My Boys* was being written was integral, like having a hovering band of kindred spirits cheering and challenging me. In addition to those authors already quoted in this book, as well as others, I was happily buoyed by Donald Miller, Ann Voskamp, Laura Winner, Skye Jethani, Sue Monk Kidd, Dietrich Bonhoeffer (including Eric Metaxas' excellent biography,

Bonhoeffer: Pastor, Martyr, Prophet, Spy), Nadia Bolz Weber, Shane Claiborne, Dieter Zander, and Michael Yankoski.

I must credit Chaim Potok's *My Name is Asher Lev* for demanding my authenticity as I wrote *Blackbirds & My Boys* and for providing me a beautiful framework within which to write about my abortion.

Having access to a breathtaking collection of books is a true gift to a bookish gal like me. I am so grateful for the "library card" and smart suggestions from Robb.

Dr. Gary, my theology professor, wrote a comment on one of my short reflection papers: "This should be published." I am so thankful for your hasty scrawling on the bottom of that page.

Pastor Mark Ashton read to his congregation a letter which I had written to him. It spoke about how my heart and my sons were impacted by the impromptu offering to single moms on that Advent Sunday which is mentioned in "Blackbirds." Thank you not only for recognizing the struggles of single moms but for sparking within me the joy and passion of writing.

Without all my Selah sisters, the seed of this book would have never sprouted. I love you all.

Too many times, I wanted to just quit writing—the enemy of our dreams can be so conniving and convincing. Sitting at a table at Sam's Dairy Queen, my friend, Leanne, spoke Spirit-drenched words of affirmation over me. Those words have prodded me along more than once!

I had no idea how desperately we writers need editors. Danica, femme and editor extraordinaire, graciously demonstrated my desperate need through her outrageous grace and detailed expertise. I find myself wanting to bake a kitchen full of cookies for her!

And speaking of outrageous grace, it is easily spotted—just look at the cover of this book! If that were not enough, just look at how fabulous this entire book looks! My sister-like friend, Kelly, is way more than an in-demand artist and graphic designer; she's also highly skilled at finding unnecessary spaces and commas in copy. She was my second editor. And I do not have enough cookie sheets.

Someone like me could have never traversed the rugged terrain of writing this book without the hand-holding, heart-hearing help of a spiritual guide. Fortunately, because of Anne, who exudes the loving, safe acceptance of Jesus, I did not have to.

Diane read every movement, as rough as some of those first drafts were, and she always urged me to keep writing. Always. Maybe I should just start a bakery.

Mama, you also read each movement. Your love energized these pages like mugs of steaming Starbucks, and your constant words of encouragement will never be forgotten. Daddy, your faithful support allowed me to write. If only there were an angelic language I could borrow to let y'all know how much I love you both.

Taylor, Zach, and Sam—the immeasurable blessing of living these stories with each of you, my sons, is the finest example of grace. Sometimes—okay, quite often—I'm sure it did not feel like grace to you! Remember the card and big box of Junior Mints you gave me when I thought this book was completed (but it was actually only half-written!)? The sweetness of your words and candy were the carbohydrates that fueled the completion of *Blackbirds & My Boys!*

It seems silly to attach only my name to this book. Jesus wrote this book with me. And I wrote it with Him. I wrote because of His unfathomable grace and His indescribable beauty.

And because of His blackbirds.